Landing Your First Real Job

Linda Linn
Certified Personnel Consultant

McGraw-Hill

New York   San Francisco   Washington, D.C.   Auckland   Bogotá
Caracas   Lisbon   London   Madrid   Mexico City   Milan
Montreal   New Delhi   San Juan   Singapore
Sydney   Tokyo   Toronto

Library of Congress catalog card number: 96-77200

McGraw-Hill

A Division of The McGraw·Hill Companies

1 2 3 4 5 6 7 8 9 0 MAL/MAL 9 0 1 0 9 8 7 6

ISBN 0-07-038061-9

*The sponsoring editor for this book was Betsy N. Brown, the assistant editor was Danielle
Munley, the editing supervisor was Fred Dahl, and the production supervisor was
Suzanne W. B. Rapcavage. It was set in Century by Inkwell Publishing Services.*

Printed and bound by Malloy Lithographers.

Graphics by Eric Gunnar Johnson.

McGraw-Hill books are available at special quantity discounts to use as premiums and sales
promotions, or for use in corporate training programs. For more information, please write to the
Director of Special Sales, McGraw-Hill, 11 West 19th Street, New York, NY 10011. Or contact
your local bookstore.

 This book is printed on acid-free paper.

This is for my kids, *Ryan* and *Tracie*.
If you learn nothing else in life, please know that dreams *do* come true.
You just have to believe in yourself
and then work hard to make them happen!

And it's also for you, *Sam Keller*.
You opened my eyes to my potential and changed my life.
There's no greater way I can thank you
than to do the same for others!

Contents

Introduction

A Job in Six Weeks?
My Promise to You

My job in this book is to help you find your first real job faster than you would on your own.

How much faster? Probably in less than two months.

I'm a recruiter who specializes in the entry-level job market. The majority of the candidates I've worked with have received an offer *within six weeks of meeting with me* for the first time. It's a commitment I make to all my clients if the individual is willing to work with me and complete all our counseling sessions.

When I tell that to people who have been pounding the pavement looking for a job for eighteen months, they usually don't believe me (even if they're too polite to say so). But the news also leaves them feeling very hopeful.

I'm not meeting with you personally, so I can't arrange interviews for you. Still, believe me, that's the easy part of the process. I know what companies want. The most challenging part of my job is improving the job-finding skills of recent graduates and introducing them to the intricacies of the entry-level market.

The expertise I have to offer, based on lots of experience with thousands of candidates and the managers who hire them, is the reason my clients usually get job offers within six weeks.

And now that expertise is available to you in *Landing Your First Real Job*.

While I can't guarantee that you will start to work within a set period after reading this book, I can promise to open your eyes to certain truths about the entry-level job market and give you techniques that will make your search less agonizing and, hopefully, much shorter.

So I extend the same commitment to you as to my clients: My job is to help you improve your self-marketing skills, increase your self-confidence, and get you closer to an offer. Your job is to land that offer.

And you will.

Acknowledgments

This book has been fun to write. But I can't say I did it all by myself. Without knowing it, all the corporate recruiters I've worked with and all the thousands of graduates I've interviewed have made contributions to this book. Without their observations, mistakes, idiosyncrasies, opinions, and basic knowledge, this book would not exist.

To those who knowingly gave their time, talent, and resources, I give special thanks. Dan Wismar, Bill Whitt, Tom Anthony, Bob Steenlage, and Mike MacNeil all contributed in their own very special ways to getting this project off the ground.

LINDA LINN

1

The Career Start-up Myth

A Degree Is No Guarantee

What am I doing wrong?

Rita lived in a small port city on Lake Erie. She went to college in Cleveland and lived on or around campus for six years while completing both her bachelor's and master's degrees and achieving above-average grades.

She worked at least 20 hours a week in a variety of positions during the school year and held down a full-time job throughout each summer at her father's land development company.

During the course of our first phone conversation I learned a lot about Rita. She had been out of school for almost a year and was continuing to work in her dad's firm. Although her position carried some weight and had above-average responsibilities for a recent graduate, she wasn't happy in it. Rita wanted to establish a career that would clearly be her own. She didn't want to be tied to her father's business and successes.

Rita went on to tell me she was looking for an opportunity that would encompass finance and real estate, her bachelor's major and minor. For almost a year she scoured her town for a suitable position. Not surprisingly, the only two interviews she had scored were through her father's connections. Both were dead ends. I could tell she was more than a little discouraged with her situation.

"I thought the idea was to go to college, work hard, get good grades, graduate on time, and have some career focus. I did all that and I still can't find a job. A lot of my friends have already started to work—and they don't even have master's degrees. The job market is bad enough and now I'm competing with fresh graduates. I'm a year out of school and I still don't have any experience. I'm reminded of that all the time. I just don't understand what I'm doing wrong."

You're not doing anything wrong.

Rita's comments about herself are familiar. I hear them all the time from recent college graduates. With variations, of course (not everybody has the problem of not wanting to work in the family business).

I'll tell you what I told Rita: *I don't think you're doing anything wrong.*

So does the problem lie in the rotten job market then? Yes and no.

GOOD NEWS

Actually, after a l-o-n-g and depressing downward spiral, entry-level job trends are looking up. More companies are interviewing and hiring on campus, and the number of first-time slots is up a bit.

Still, as I tell my clients, you can't live your life according to economic trends. Even the most favorable conditions can't help you as much as *you can help yourself.*

Rita's problem, and maybe yours, is that she just doesn't know what to do. Her education prepared her for any number of careers, but it did virtually nothing to prepare her for the job market and particularly for the interviews that lie ahead. (I have a bone to pick with colleges about that, and you should too. But we'll discuss that later.)

Like most of my clients, Rita believed that her degree, particularly her master's degree, would guarantee her a good job. After searching for several months, she found that getting her career started after graduation was not automatic. Her degree was no guarantee. And neither is yours.

Facing the realities of the job market

I can't count how many recent college graduates I've interviewed over the past six years, but the number is probably in the thousands.

Some come to me while the ink is still wet on their diplomas, but most are in Rita's shoes. They've been out of school for anywhere from six months to three years and are still trying to land their first "real" job.

TRAPS TO AVOID

"The mass of men lead lives of quiet desperation," said Henry David Thoreau. Substitute "job hunters" for "the mass of men" and I would agree completely!

But it doesn't have to be that way. Anxiety quickly becomes destructive. It starts eating you up inside, employers sense it, rejection sets in, and the vicious cycle escalates.

You can nip job search anxiety in the bud. Reading this book is a good way to start.

No matter how long they've been job hunting, when clients first come to me, they communicate a kind of despair.

Those feelings are not only normal, but are very understandable. On average, 1.8 million people graduate from colleges across this country each year. Those are some pretty big numbers, especially when you realize they are all considered entry-level candidates and are competing for positions in a job market that is small in comparison to the market for those with experience.

On top of that, unless your college was the exception rather than the rule, it taught you zip about marketing yourself and doing well in interviews. Job interviews are an especially tough place to learn through trial and error. It's a little like sticking an inexperienced pilot behind the controls of a moving airplane and saying "Good luck!"

It can be tough enough just to land an interview. To get one and then lose out on an opportunity because you blew the interview—that's a real reason to be discouraged. But it won't happen to you after you read Chapters 10, 11, and 12 of this book and put in some time honing your interviewing skills.

Don't throw in the towel!

All things considered, your job search can get a little depressing. But don't give up yet. There is hope, and lots of it.

If you're reading this book, you already realize you need some help in finding a job. I can provide that help, but your attitude and level of motivation will determine your success in landing the job offer.

Keep in mind what I pointed out at the very beginning of this book. Just about all my entry-level clients get offers within six weeks. Hang on to that fact. Keep it in your mind's eye and recall it when the going gets rough.

There is really no "magic" about how I guide you through the job search process, or, to be more specific, how I teach you to guide yourself. It all stems from experience I've gained from people who have been there before (and not long before). Through literally thousands of conversations with college graduates, I've been able to pinpoint specific problems, obstacles, and hurdles others have encountered along the way.

I've listened to them express their feelings and their frustrations, and I've developed a unique understanding of what they are faced with when playing the interviewing game.

I know what employers want.

There are two sides to every story, as the saying goes, and my job as a recruiter is to understand both sides.

I've sat on the other side of the desk and dealt with hundreds of companies. I've put in thousands of hours of phone time and face-to-face time with the human resource managers, college recruiters, and department managers who do the interviewing and hiring. And I've gotten their perspective on what they want and don't want in a candidate.

WAKE-UP CALL

What employers look for in a candidate is not just job skills, but qualities such as personality, attitude, poise, communication skills, and appearance.

"Hey!" you may be saying. "I'm looking for work, not for first prize in a personality contest!"

True. But that doesn't change the reality that people hire people, not grade point averages and degrees, and that's the reality you're faced with in your job search.

Here's another thing to consider. As a professional go-between, I have the benefit of hearing employers' feedback after each and every interview. And I'm not shy about asking them questions. The tips and techniques I offer you are based on years of probing, of hearing directly from employers what works in an interview and what doesn't.

If one of my candidates bombs in an interview, I learn why. And I make sure that person—or any other client—learns how to handle things differently if confronted with a similar situation.

If it's not real-life, you won't find it here.

You'll find many real-life experiences in these pages. Although I've changed the names, all of the stories I'll share with you are true stories of real-life problems, real-life people, and real-life solutions.

You should know that my recruiting experience has been mainly within the realm of the Fortune 500 in service and manufacturing industries. However, my advice on marketing and interviewing crosses all job search boundaries, guaranteed. Whether you're following a career path in social service, education, medicine, government, or business, you still need to interview well and project self-confidence in order to be a successful prospect for employment.

Before moving on, let's catch up with Rita and see what happened to her.

Rita had limited her job search to her hometown because of her love of sailing. Being an avid enthusiast and competitor in the sport, she wanted to remain close to the lake. Although it seemed obvious to me that relocating would open doors for her, she had given it little thought.

During counseling I suggested the possibility of other port cities that would support both her career ambitions and her desire to keep sailing. She agreed to consider them, and together we selected several major East Coast cities to target. We were successful in landing her several interviews, one of them with USF&G, a major property-casualty insurance company.

Rita made the trip to their headquarters in Baltimore and interviewed for a position as a real estate management trainee. She spent the entire day there, had several interviews within the organization, got the grand tour of their facilities, and returned home that night feeling like a different person.

Within days, the company called me to extend Rita an official job offer with a starting salary of $30,000, much higher than the entry-level norm.

Rita asked the company for a few days to think about the offer. By the end of the week she phoned me to say she was turning down the job.

It seems that when Rita's boyfriend of four years heard that she might move to Baltimore, he proposed marriage on the spot. She said "yes" to him and "no" to the company.

Personally, I didn't view the situation as a failure. To me, it was a success. I could see a marked improvement in Rita's attitude and outlook once she completed the counseling and had a couple of quality interviews. She was much more confident and hopeful about her career prospects.

Rita took what she learned about marketing and interviewing and, with a renewed optimism, remarketed herself to local employers. Eventually, she landed a career position through her own efforts in a field that interested her. It did pay considerably less than she would have earned in Baltimore, but it was close to the lake and, of course, to her fiancé.

She found the new job on her own, by the way. In less than six weeks.

LOOKING AHEAD

Just as a degree is no guarantee of a job, a job offer in another city is no guarantee that your college sweetheart will pop the question!

Still, it's worth thinking about how your personal life might change after you get the job offer you want.

2

Planning Ahead

Damage Control ...
The Consequences of Poor Planning

A waiter's tale

When Beau came to me he was 29 years old and had just completed his MBA. He wanted a position as a financial analyst and thought I could deliver the goods.

During our first interview I learned that he had been going to school, off and on, for the past ten years. During that time he had worked for only two employers—both upscale restaurants where he was a waiter.

Beau certainly wasn't a job hopper. He had pretty decent grades, a 2.8 in his BS and a 3.4 in his MBA. There were no internships or extracurriculars in his background and his transcripts were four pages long because he had changed majors and transferred among colleges so many times. On the plus side, he had developed great communication skills from dealing with the public, and was very self-confident and money-motivated—traits that are typical of good waiters.

He had begun his career search three months prior to graduating and was already in despair over not being able to land an interview, let alone a job. He came to me for help.

Unfortunately, what I had to tell him was not what he wanted to hear.

Beau had some prices to pay for the way he handled his college career. He never gave any thought to how prospective employers might view the management of his career planning. And that's what college is ... career planning. That is why Beau chose to attend college in the first place: He knew he didn't want to wait tables for the rest of his life.

WAKE-UP CALL

Beau didn't realize a basic truth about job hunting, which is: Once you start interviewing, employers are going to be just as interested in *how you got your degree* as they are in the fact that you have one at all.

Optimal career planning meets real career planning.

Ideally, career planning should start during the freshman year (of college, not high school—although that may be something to think about). Realistically, it rarely does. If it did, I'd see lots of perfect-looking resumes and transcripts, and I don't.

At least that is something to ease your mind: You're competing against very few fellow college graduates with perfect credentials and flawless college careers. Like Beau, almost all students create obstacles for themselves during college. When he started interviewing he learned the true meaning of "If I only knew then what I know now." Soon that old sentiment may seem like less of a cliche to you, too. It might even be a fresh new discovery.

Unfortunate mistakes and how employers perceive them

College students often make some typical mistakes while pursuing their educations and are unenlightened about how employers view them.

"Mistakes" may be too strong a word, because you never set out to sabotage yourself. Call them fumbles, bad circumstances, rash decisions, or unfortunate moves. The point is that they merit close examination for two reasons:

- They almost always end up raising eyebrows in interviews.
- They are frequently cited as reasons for rejection.

When you know up front what's facing you, you're better prepared to cope with the problem down the line. And the more you understand things from the employer's perspective, the readier you are to overcome self-generated obstacles.

LOOKING AHEAD

If you're still in school or are about to enter, I especially urge you to take this advice to heart. Study these common mistakes and their likely consequences, and steer clear. It will help you avoid damage control four or five years from now.

Unfortunate move #1: Taking too long to graduate

I had to turn Beau away as a recruitment client because of the ten years it took him to graduate.

I'm not an ogre. I admire people who pursue a degree, work for it, and stick with it. But harsh reality sometimes dictates the shots.

At the time Beau called me, I did not represent one single company that would grant interviews to people who took more than six

WAKE-UP CALL

There is one question you cannot escape: "How long did it take you to earn your degree?"

It's one of the first things that employers ask a recruiter about an entry-level candidate. And if they don't ask the recruiter, it's guaranteed they'll ask *you* in the interview.

years to complete their degrees. (We're talking about degrees typically earned in four years, of course, not longer programs like pharmacology or veterinary medicine.)

After the fifth or sixth year, the windows of opportunity begin to close. The longer you take to graduate, the fewer windows remain open.

Why is this such a burning issue with employers? It is of particular importance if you are interviewing for a training program, for one thing. Rightly or not, an employer assumes it will take twice as long to train you as another candidate, since it took you almost twice as long to get your degree.

You've probably heard the phrase "goal-oriented" so often it makes you choke, but employers recruit goal-oriented candidates. They want people who are eager to complete training and start working on the job. And even if no training program is involved, they still want candidates whose goal is to advance.

Every rule has its exceptions, but if you've taken more than six years to graduate, you may need to lower your expectations somewhat. The choicest plums may be out of reach, but you can still find offers worth plucking. Obstacles *can* be overcome.

Realistically, because it took you longer to get your degree, it might take you a little longer to get where you want to go careerwise.

Strategies for Beau. As you'll recall, Beau's goal was to be a financial analyst in the banking industry. Right up front, I told him he would have to get there the hard way. He was up against candidates with well-rounded college careers who had graduated in four or five years.

But if you want something badly enough, there are ways to get it. I advised Beau to get in the door as a teller or customer service rep with an organization that promotes from within. He should apply himself, establish a reputation as a good employee, and work his way up through the ranks. This route would take longer, but then so had he!

Beau balked at this, as you might imagine. He felt I was telling him to lower his standards and, in a way, I was. But we agreed it would be even less appealing to wait tables for another year while a banking career slipped farther out of reach.

I suggested an alternative. Since Beau had worked in the restaurant industry for so many years, he knew the business well and might want to put his degree to work in a familiar environment. The restaurant Beau worked for was part of a chain. At my urging, he went to their corporate offices to inquire about internal audit and bookkeeping positions. The employer already knew him to be a reliable, hard-working, conscientious employee. They also knew he had been going to college the entire time he was working for them and had now completed his degree.

Even though there were no positions open at the time, it was only a few months before Beau was called to interview for an audit position. He got the job and is now building his credentials in financial analysis. He may someday get the position in banking he wanted all along.

So don't lose hope even if you did take a long time to graduate. Just remember to keep your expectations in line with your credentials and be prepared to pay the price for taking the extra time.

How important are degrees, majors, and transcripts? The length of your college career was probably determined by the degree or program you ultimately pursued. If you changed your major more than twice, it's almost a given that you've tacked an extra semester or two onto your college career. The same holds true if you switched from a liberal arts curriculum to the sciences or vice versa.

First of all, your major and degree don't necessarily define your career goals. There are a lot of people out there in corporate America who started their careers in fields totally unrelated to their major fields of study. It's true even in fields that seem straight and narrow. Just because you have an accounting degree doesn't automatically mean you're going to be an accountant.

In my opinion, it usually does more harm to switch majors than it does to, let's say, stick with accounting even though you discover in your third year that your interests lie more in finance or marketing. It's better to graduate on time with an accounting major and take night classes in marketing while pursuing that field than it is to take six years to get a marketing degree.

Unfortunate move #2: Changing your major too often

The majority of my clients changed their major at least once. That tells me universities need to offer more career guidance to freshmen and sophomores. Actually, some of the more progressive learning institutions do offer first-year classes for credit to help students define their career paths. Unfortunately, not enough students take advantage of them.

TRAPS TO AVOID

The attitude I observe is, "Well, I have at least four years to make up my mind as to what I want to do." *Wrong.* The sooner you commit to a degree and major, the less time it takes you to graduate.

If you're reading this and are still in school and have decided to change your major, take summer classes to pick up the slack and make up the necessary credits. That way, you'll still graduate in a reasonable time and will telegraph a high degree of drive and initiative to potential employers.

Another consequence of not committing to and sticking with your course of study is that you come across to an employer as a candidate who lacks focus. I know you might think that's an unfair assumption, but I'm only reporting what companies tell me.

Consder the employer's point of view. If you changed your major three times, your potential employer is wondering if you're going to change your mind about your career path nine months into the training program. Companies tie up a lot of time and money in trainees. They are rightfully concerned about your willingness to stick with the position long enough to give them a return on their investment.

If transcripts could talk ... Another thing to remember about changing your major, and your mind, is that these moves become a permanent part of your academic record. Your transcripts don't lie. If you started out in pre-med and flunked out, then switched to engineering and struggled and ended up in communications, your transcripts tell the employer the whole story. You don't have to.

The majority of college graduates don't realize how important those transcripts are until they have to start passing out copies in interviews. If an employer requests transcripts, especially early in the interview process, be prepared to provide explanations for any fails, withdrawals, or transfers.

Like most students, you probably didn't give it much thought when you decided to drop a class during your sophomore year because you had a personality conflict with the professor or you were a little overloaded on credits. Now you're sitting in interviews and discovering

WAKE-UP CALL

Why do employers care so much about failed classes or withdrawals? Isn't that ancient history?

Not to them. They assume you have poor planning skills, a poor work ethic, an inability to finish what you start, or poor decision-making skills. These are all negatives in a prospective employee.

There are some legitimate reasons for class withdrawals. "The prof was a jerk" is not one of them. Lying is not a good strategy either.

Chapters 10 through 13 have to do with interviewing. If your college records resemble swiss cheese, study those chapters with special care.

all of a sudden that the classes you withdrew from during your sophomore year are a big issue with potential employers.

For those of you still in college or planning to return for an advanced degree, two ways to avoid those unnecessary "w"s are to select your courses carefully and to avoid overloading semester hours. Taking too many classes almost always results in early withdrawals, failures, or, worse yet, lower grades overall. The more "w"s you have on your transcripts, the more explaining you'll have to do in interviews.

Unfortunate move #3: Not making the greatest grades

Right off the bat, I'll assure you that low grades don't mean the end of your chances for a challenging career.

There are some careers and areas of study in which grade point average has a definite impact on whether or not you get the interview, much less the job. This is particularly true of so-called "application majors." Accounting, statistics, math, actuarial sciences, and computer sciences are a few examples.

In these areas of study, the skills you learn in the classroom are exactly the same skills you'll be using on the job. If your applied skills in the classroom were below average, the employer can (and will) assume your performance on the job would be below average as well.

When applying for positions of this nature, your GPA will definitely be a factor. In most cases, employers require at least a 3.0 but more often look for one that is even higher.

Take heart, though. Many recruiters, myself included, do not measure candidates by their GPAs.

A GPA of 2.7 or lower can be, and most likely will be, an obstacle in the interview. Prepare to offer an explanation. If it's valid, you'll most likely overcome the employer's objection. Some explanations that I've seen succeed: You worked more than 15 to 20 hours a week. You were active in clubs and organizations (and I don't mean party-crazy frats). You carried extra semester hours in order to graduate earlier.

GOOD NEWS

Frankly, I'd rather represent someone with a 2.7 GPA who held down a job, helped to pay tuition, and got involved in extracurriculars, than a person who carried a 3.8 GPA and did nothing but study to keep the grades up. A more well-rounded candidate is usually a more versatile candidate.

Unfortunate move #4: The one-track college career

I wish I had a chance to talk to every college freshman in order to convince them of the importance of a well-rounded education. Planning your college career involves so much more than selecting classes, showing up, and turning in your assignments.

More and more these days, employers want people who have enhanced their education with jobs, extracurricular activities, and those very important internships. Without doubt, my hottest and most marketable candidates are those who have managed to juggle education, employment, community service, and social activities.

If you weren't active on campus or didn't hold down a job of any kind, I can almost guarantee you that employers will bring up the subject in an interview. Even if they don't raise the issue, believe me when I tell you that they're still thinking about it. Out loud or silently, they are questioning your motivation, initiative, and work ethic.

It's that real-life perspective again. Participation in extracurricular activities helps college students develop necessary job skills not taught in a classroom. Communication, people skills, working in a team environment, and the ability to handle multiple tasks are lessons learned by doing. Reading a book and writing an essay on leadership doesn't make you a leader.

If yours was a one-track college career, it's not too late to do something about it. Of course you can't go back and join a service organization and you can't invent a job for yourself in college if you didn't have one. But you *can* start today on making up the lost ground.

Get active while you're conducting your career search. Contact your college, find out about joining organizations related to your major, and get involved in alumni work. It'll be much easier to answer those objections if employers know you are trying to compensate for what you now realize is a void in your educational background.

Get a job!   My universal suggestion to job seekers is to get a job, *any* job. I don't care if you are living at home and Mom and Dad are footing the bill while you pound the pavement. Get a job!

From an employer's point of view, you convey a much stronger attitude and work ethic when you're willing to work for $5 or $6 an hour than when you're taking the easy road—i.e., allowing your parents to continue to support you during your job search.

Maybe you're thinking the same thing my clients do: "If I get a job I won't have time to look for one, right?"

Wrong, wrong, wrong. I just don't buy that. Neither do the employers who hire college graduates. There are lots of hourly positions that offer the flexibility you'll need in order to look for a career while holding down a job.

In fact, when you apply for work, let the employer know up front that you view the job as temporary for now. Restaurants, landscaping companies, and retail stores are just a few types of businesses that welcome reliable employees, even if only on a part-time basis.

GOOD NEWS

When you lay your cards on the table about needing a flexible schedule for interviews, most employers understand. If you come through for them, they'll be willing to work with you.

Is your potential employer clearly unreceptive to the idea? Better to find out before you make each other miserable. Keep looking until you find an employer who understands your situation and is willing to provide a flexible work schedule. They do exist.

Internships: It's never too late.   An internship will pay off in a big way. If you're fortunate enough to have secured one in college, it will be a definite plus in your job search.

Internships aren't always easy to come by and employers know that. Landing an internship usually requires research, hard work, good time management, motivation, and initiative. They sometimes require sacrifice, since quite a few intern programs offer class credit and no pay. Having an internship to your credit sends a lot of positive messages about you to the employer, in addition to giving you several months of exposure to the industry and profession you're pursuing.

Lack of internships usually won't work against you, but having them does provide a measurable edge in a competitive market. My advice is that it's never too late. Even if you're two years out of college, you can still pursue internships. You will have missed out on the opportunity to gain class credit, but you'll still benefit in all the ways I've mentioned.

Treat the search for an internship as if you're searching for a job. Target any company that interests you or is related to your potential career. Approach them with the idea that, as part of your career planning, you'd like to intern with them for several months in exchange for

FIXING MISTAKES

By pursuing an internship after graduation, you display focus and maturity that can make up for a lot of other mistakes you may have made in the process of getting your degree.

And who knows? Your efforts could very well lead to an offer, or at the very least, to being put on the payroll while you're interning.

the corporate exposure. If you *really* want to get their attention and increase the odds of acceptance, offer to do it for *free*. Putting in 10 to 15 hours a week gratis is a small price to pay for the benefits you'll reap.

By investing yourself in a project like this during your job search you'll build a better resume, gain self-confidence, and garner new experience. In addition, it's a chance to strengthen your communication skills and polish your interviewing style, which will make you even more marketable.

Myths about master's degrees

If you ask 100 people about the merits of pursuing a master's degree, you will probably get 100 different opinions.

My observations are not arbitrary, but are based on my years of experience in recruiting college graduates for Fortune 500 companies. If you're interested in getting into the business world, what I have to share with you may prove valuable in making a decision about continuing your education. For those who already have a master's degree, this might shed some light on how you're perceived in the marketplace.

Grab your sunglasses; this light is pretty harsh.

WAKE-UP CALL

Based on the responses of the employers I work with, I find that initially a master's degree is more often an albatross than an advantage in your career search.

Sure, some positions and companies require an advanced degree, but I'm talking about the majority. And not only do the majority *not require* an advanced degree, a lot of the recruiters actually *shy away from* master's candidates.

Why? The problem lies not with the degree itself, but with some typical attitudes that arise in the process of securing the degree. Other significant objections center around *why* you pursued a master's degree and *what* you assume it will do for you.

As a master's candidate, you can expect employers to question you carefully about your motivation and expectations. Don't be surprised if they are scrutinized.

Check out the following "Master's Myths" for a better understanding of what I mean.

Master's myth #1: "I'll make more money with a master's degree."

Typically, master's candidates have unrealistic salary expectations. It might surprise you to know that the majority of employers show no salary preference to a master's candidate at the entry level. As far as they're concerned, you are still a trainee with little or no experience in the field and you'll require the same amount of corporate training as an individual with a four-year degree. So why should they pay you any more? The bottom line is that it's going to cost the company the same amount of money to train you both, whether you have a master's degree or a four-year degree.

Master's myth #2: "With a master's degree I'll be given increased job responsibilities upon entering a training program."

Again, you have no more experience than the person with the bachelor's degree. In fact, the person with the four-year degree might have strong leadership and management skills developed through participation in extracurriculars, athletics, and work history. If you have a master's degree and nothing to go with it, the other candidate is more qualified to assume additional responsibilities upon entering the training program.

When interviewing a candidate with a master's degree, most recruiters will eventually get around to asking what the motivation was for pursuing the advanced degree. If your answer has anything at all to do with myths #1 and #2, I can guarantee that the employer will question your attitude and expectations and, quite possibly, use them as a reason to eliminate you from consideration.

The track record shows that a master's candidate who has unrealistic expectations about earnings and job responsibilities often becomes the "problem child" of the training program. This is particularly true in situations in which the companies hire more than one trainee at a time and the candidates are trained in groups or classroom environments.

Master's myth #3: "I'll get my master's degree now because the job market will probably be better two years from now."

Oh, *please*, don't fall for that one!

When asked in an interview about your motivation for pursuing an advanced degree, this might very well be the worst possible answer you can give.

If you are truly motivated to go to work after graduating, you will. Granted, it's not easy landing your first career position. It takes time, hard work, and perseverance. If, after three months (and remember, the average job search takes nine to twelve months!) you don't get an offer and you throw in the towel, the employer's perception is that you are a quitter, you lack motivation, and you are unable to set and achieve goals.

Master's myth #4: "I'll get my master's degree now because that way I can defer my student loans."

Many of you who use the "better job market in two years" excuse for getting your master's degrees actually returned to college to defer your student loans.

Financial situations can be tough, no doubt about it. Employers realize that. Still, regardless of whether you buy into master's myth #3 or #4, you raise crucial questions on the part of the employer. When met with adversity in the training program, will you give up as easily or will you stick with your course of action in order to achieve your goals? Will you run away from your responsibilities in the job and avoid facing difficult issues?

To find work worth having, these are questions you must address.

Getting your master's degree the right way

If you are truly interested in completing a master's degree, why not invest your time and energy in securing a position with a corporation that will pay for it? Now, that's advanced thinking.

A lot of big companies, and some smaller ones as well, encourage higher education. Yours will be a lot more meaningful to you *and* the company if you take classes in the evenings and take what you learn in the books to work with you the next day. You benefit by getting your education this way and so do the employers. Why else would they be so willing to pick up the tab?

I've said this before but it's worth repeating. *How* and *why* you pursued your degree are often more important than the fact that you earned one.

3

Your Personal Inventory

Sizing Yourself Up for the Market

Andrea paid her way through school by waiting on tables, life-guarding, and giving swimming lessons. During our career counseling sessions, we completed a personal inventory that opened her eyes to several strengths she didn't realize she had.

Andrea told me she always made more tips and did her best work during peak restaurant hours. Many food servers are at their worst then. So there was strength #1—the ability to work well under pressure.

Andrea casually mentioned that she often filled in for the hostess or cashier when they called in sick or were running late. This signaled additional new strengths: Andrea was obviously multitask oriented and could learn new jobs quickly and easily.

As a lifeguard at the same pool for four consecutive summers, Andrea was given additional responsibilities each year. Eventually she was scheduling and managing the activities of four other lifeguards, ordering and inventorying all pool supplies and chemicals, and helping to organize and conduct classes in CPR.

Yet Andrea discounted that job ("I was just a lifeguard") and even omitted it from her resume. When she took a closer look at what she had done, she discovered she had the potential for management, good organizational and planning skills, and the ability to work in a team environment while rising to a level of leadership.

To earn money by giving swimming lessons, Andrea drummed up business by posting notices and networking at local schools and country clubs. Soon business was coming to her, thanks to great word-of-mouth advertising. What I saw here was a strong goal orientation, self-motivation, an excellent work ethic, and the ability to manage the activities of others.

Andrea was a marketing major with an average GPA and few extracurricular activities. Yet she had no problem landing a job as a marketing research assistant with MCI. Her strengths fit the job description perfectly, despite a lackluster academic career and no "direct" job experience.

What's important is that Andrea had the potential and could prove it. The employer provided the training, and now Andrea is on the road to success in her field.

Deciding on your career path can be one of the most difficult and challenging tasks you've ever confronted. It involves evaluating who you are, what's important to you, what you're capable of accomplishing, what your shortcomings might be, and where you want your career to take you. Just a few small things!

Andrea's personal inventory helped her answer some of those questions, and so will yours. What you discover about yourself during this exercise will help point you in the right direction for a successful career. It will also better prepare you for the job market and the interviewing grind.

Taking a personal inventory is a simple matter of listing and defining your strengths and weaknesses (if you call that "simple"). The real work lies in what you *do* with what you find out about yourself.

The actual inventory appears later in this chapter. For now, I want to emphasize the benefits of going through the process.

Think of your personal inventory as a resource. The better you know yourself, the better and more successful you'll be in securing your first career position, not to mention mapping out the right career.

LOOKING AHEAD

The secret of your success in this exercise is to evaluate yourself candidly and thoroughly. Be totally honest with yourself and about your skills. The payoff is well worth the effort. Your personal inventory will help you:

- establish career focus.
- develop interviewing sales tools.
- increase your self-confidence.
- improve your interviewing skills.

Establishing career focus: What should you be when you grow up?

In my practice, I don't see many college grads who can confidently state what career path they intend to follow. That's reasonable. How would they know? They have no experience. They have very limited knowledge of the job market and they have been given little, if any, education in occupational job descriptions.

So what do you want to be when you grow up? If you don't know, the following concept might help.

THE SUITABILITY PRINCIPLE

A graduate will be most successful in a career that maximizes the individual's strengths and avoids stressing the individual's weaknesses.

Simple? Very simple?

Obvious? Painfully obvious?

Absolutely. But why is this simple, obvious concept so often overlooked?

Based on my research with thousands of recent college graduates, I've observed that more than 75 percent have quit their first postgraduation job within the first year. Why? My guess is their lack of success is directly linked to their lack of suitability to the job description.

Your primary purpose in taking a personal inventory is to determine your suitability to the career opportunities available to a recent grad. The more attuned you are to your actual and potential strengths, the greater the odds are that you'll make a better career choice for yourself.

Sounds pretty easy, doesn't it? Find a career whose job description asks you to do, each and every day, what comes most naturally and easily to you. Equally important, you'll learn to stay away from the careers that will tax your weaknesses.

Every career opportunity has a job description, a list of half a dozen or more tasks that are performed on a daily, or near-daily, basis. Every graduate comes equipped with a list of strengths, or things that come easily to them. Those strengths either are inherent or have been developed through previous training and conditioning.

If you lack suitability for a position, if it stresses your weaknesses, the likelihood is that you will struggle or fail. You'll become part of that unhappy 75 percent who are disillusioned with themselves and their first postgraduation job.

On the flip side, if the job description is one that utilizes your strengths, then good things will happen. Your progress will be swifter. You'll be recognized and promoted for your efforts. Your salary will increase as your responsibilities grow. And you'll feel good about yourself for succeeding at the job!

Of course, taking your personal inventory is just the first step in this process. You also have to learn the job descriptions. I'll give you some help with that in Chapter 14, but for now, the focus is on *you*.

WAKE-UP CALL

It makes no difference how much a career opportunity pays, what the growth opportunities are, where it's located, how stable the company is, or what the job title is. *Your primary concern should be the job description and whether or not you're well suited for it.*

I stress this because your first job out of college can be the most important. You're literally building the foundation on which your career will take off and grow. If your strengths are suited to the job description, the odds are in your favor that you'll experience success.

Establishing your career focus early in the game will ultimately get you farther, faster in corporate America.

Develop interviewing sales tools: In an interview, everyone's a salesperson!

Interviewing is selling. It's true for everyone. Even if you've never sold so much as a box of Girl Scout cookies, you're going to have to learn how to sell yourself to an employer in order to land a job.

Your objective in an interview is to sell the employer on the reasons why you fit the job description and company profile. Your job is to convince the employer you have the strengths and necessary skills to do the job well.

Any salesperson who has been in the field for any length of time has developed tools for "moving" the product. The first tool is to know your product inside and out; the second is to determine the customer's needs. You then use your knowledge to convince the customer that the product has *everything* the customer needs, wants, and desires.

Imagine that you're selling a pocket knife with 15 different gizmos that do everything from clipping nails to scaling fish to threading needles. Each time you begin a sale, your first task is to learn the customer's uses for your product. By chatting a bit, you learn that Mr. Potential Buyer does not sew and has never touched a fish in his life. Let's say he needs only seven of the fifteen gizmos. You have a polished sales pitch for all fifteen, naturally, but you'll focus your energy on selling only the seven that interest this customer.

The same principles apply when you walk into an interview. The interviewer is the buyer. You are the salesperson and your skills are the gizmos on the pocketknife. You'll need to know the job description and what strengths are necessary to perform well. Just what are the employer's needs? Your task is to focus on selling your strengths that correspond to the position being filled.

Your strengths are your sales tools. The more you have and are able to prove, the more attractive a candidate you'll be. If you lay claim to fifteen strengths, like the knife salesperson, you won't talk about all fifteen. You'll focus your attention on the strengths required by this particular employer and job.

Naturally, the more strengths you've developed over the years, the more job descriptions you'll fit. Knowing your strengths and developing them into sales tools will broaden your career choices and dramatically improve your interviewing skills.

A good salesperson is a good listener. Even if you research the position and job description you might not know all there is to know about the opportunity. Learn to listen to your interviewers. It's likely they will give you a lot of information regarding their company, industry, or job description that you didn't have when you walked in the door. *When you hear a point being made that ties into one of your strengths, take the ini-*

TRAPS TO AVOID

Most recent graduates allow themselves to be *led* through an interview. They speak only when spoken to. They take little initiative in the conversation. Usually, it's because they don't know what to talk about.

They seem passive.

Nobody wants a jabbering job candidate who doesn't know when to stop talking. But your personal inventory will help you avoid the equally deadly "silent syndrome."

When you know what the employer is looking for and you're confident of what you have to offer, the interview becomes a simple matter of making the connection with words.

tiative to make the employer aware of the connection. It's called selling yourself. It's called an exchange of information.

If you are comfortable with your strengths, you'll be more confident in your presentation and you'll communicate much more effectively in the interview.

Having the strength is crucial, but it's not enough. You must also be able to *sell* the employer on the fact that you have it.

Increased self-confidence: Ready for the 15-minute test?

When I take my clients through this preliminary exercise, I see amazing transformations take place.

I start by putting them alone in an office and telling them they have 15 minutes to list as many of their strengths as they can.

It might surprise you to know the average number listed is five. We start with those and build from there. After three hours or so, the list usually grows to a dozen or more!

Try this yourself right now. Stop reading, pick up a pen and paper, and give yourself 15 minutes to list your strengths. When you've finished, tuck your list into the back of the book and go on reading this chapter and the next one.

Then, after finishing Chapter 4, take your list out and work on it again. I can almost guarantee your results will be as successful and ego-building as those of my clients. Give it a try.

Being fully aware of your strengths and your potential fit to a job opening, you can walk into the interview with a sense of "self." And when you know the job description, it's easier for you to pinpoint and discuss the skills you possess that match the specific job duties.

When you start your inventory, keep in mind that your strengths are sometimes hidden or are in the developmental stages. Just like Andrea, you'll have to dig deep and think hard. Unearth all those resources you've developed over the last twenty-odd years.

Here's the bottom line. A personal inventory goes a long way toward making you a better interviewee. You'll become more self-assured, self-confident, poised, mature, and focused. You'll know *what* to say and you'll learn *when* to say it.

Your sales tools will sell the employer on your product, namely you. Your level of preparedness will show in the interview and will help set you apart from your competition.

So, now that you know why your personal inventory is so important, let's get started.

Taking your personal inventory—Here's how it works.

First, remember this: *Honesty* is the key to success in evaluating your strengths and weaknesses.

Never kid yourself. Keep in mind that you'll have to back up each strength with a real-life experience that proves to the employer you are what you say you are.

The idea, basically, is to put your money where your mouth is. And the most effective way is to cite experiences from your *work history,* wherever possible. Avoid school-related examples, unless they somehow set you apart from the crowd. Talking about classes, professors, case studies, and campus activities will only remind employers that you're just like everyone else they've interviewed.

Also, don't *limit* yourself to experiences from work or school. It's fine to talk about all facets of your life in an interview.

A case in point is Heidi. She was a dancer who dreamt of joining a regional ballet troupe. She spent years taking lessons, practicing, and making sacrifices in order to qualify. Being a ballerina has nothing to do with being a trainee in the corporate world. But Heidi's proven goal orientation, hard work, and self-discipline are qualities employers seek in any potential candidate.

DAMAGE CONTROL

It's natural to make statements like this: "I think I'd do well in this position because I work very well under pressure and am able to manage my time effectively."

Whenever you find yourself saying or writing that, hasten to add more. To the employer, your claim alone is an empty promise. You must offer an example or situation that provides *proof.* And it should be the right kind of example. Read on to see what I mean.

Before starting your personal inventory, you need to think about one extremely crucial point.

TRAPS TO AVOID

Don't confuse your strengths and weaknesses with your likes and dislikes!

I love to ski. But every time I do it, I get battered and bruised. Skiing is *not* one of my strengths, just something I *like* to do.

Many clients tell me they'd like to get into sales because they like working with people. That's nice. Getting along well with people is an essential ingredient for success in just about any career. But it won't make you a good salesperson.

Ego drive, empathy, goal orientation, self-motivation, and the ability to take the initiative are the key strengths necessary to succeed in sales. No matter how much you'd *like* to be a sales trainee, unless you possess those qualities, you'll probably struggle to succeed.

Here's my general rule for interviewees: If you claim to possess a particular strength but can't prove it with an example of an actual experience, then I assume you're talking about something you'd *like* to do but are not actually *suited* to do.

Copy this on an index card. Hang it on your computer monitor, your bathroom mirror, or the dashboard of your car:

If you can't prove the strength, you don't own the strength!

Your personal inventory

Part 1: Job strengths checklist

As you read through this 17-point checklist, always ask yourself which experiences or jobs will back up what you want to say about yourself in an interview. My goal is to make you think a little harder about that crucial connection and to remind you that you have much more to offer than you may realize.

It *is* a huge task to evaluate yourself honestly and to determine which of these qualities you possess. Some of them may still be in the "budding stage" at this point in your life, but that's okay. A corporate training program is designed to draw on your potential and provide the polish necessary to help you develop these skills to a higher degree.

So let's get down to business.

YOUR PERSONAL INVENTORY, PART 1

1. **Do you work well independently?** Can you complete a job or task without needing or wanting a lot of close immediate supervision?

   Try to recall all the jobs you've held. Were you normally in situations that required you to work on your own? Did you rely heavily on your supervisor for your daily agenda? Were you able to manage your own time on the job or did that require the assistance of your manager?

2. **Do you take the initiative?** Do you take on new or additional assignments with little or no prodding? Do you ask for help when needed?

   Recruiters like graduates who take the initiative. Your willingness to take the initiative will be reflected in your level of preparedness for the interview. How you communicate and sell yourself in the interview also demonstrates your initiative.

   If you are able to move from one assignment to the next in the workplace without being prompted by your supervisor, then let the employer know that. Also let the employer know that, if met with an obstacle, you would not hesitate to request help from someone more experienced.

3. **Do you work well under pressure?** We all work under pressure from time to time. But, do you work *better* when the heat is on?

   Restaurant work, customer service and sales jobs during the Christmas season, and any quota-oriented jobs would all help back up your claims about yourself in this area.

4. **Are you goal-oriented?** Do you set goals for yourself, either personal or professional, and work toward achieving them?

   Aside from the fact that you graduated from college, think about some goals that you've set in your life. What was the purpose? How did you go about meeting these goals? Were you successful or did you fall short? If you failed, how did you feel about it? Did you try again?

   Employers love goal-oriented trainees. In interviews, you can expect very specific questions about your goals. You need to be prepared with your answers.

5. **Are you achievement-oriented?** Many people set goals but aren't always able, or motivated, to achieve them. Look at all the New Year's resolutions that have been long forgotten by February.

When you resolve to do something, do you follow through? Are you able to work with a sense of urgency and do you have a strong desire to finish what you start? Think of some of your most noteworthy achievements and be prepared to talk about them in interviews.

6. **Are you a team player?** Teamwork is on the upswing in corporate America today. I'm referring to teams of people who are working together (or "cross-functionally," in current jargon) on a project or goal, *not* the gang that meets after work for softball. Can *you* work well with a group of people trying to achieve a common goal?

GOOD NEWS

Teamwork is an area where you may have a real advantage over a more experienced candidate. Many people have only worked in the old "me boss, you employee" job hierarchy, and it's hard for them to make the switch.

Any team sports, clubs, organizations, or community service activities in which you participated will help to sell this very important strength to an employer.

7. **Do you possess leadership qualities?** Do you tend to take charge in group situations?

If you were ever elected to positions of responsibility, or appointed captain or co-captain of an athletic team, you most likely have the potential to become a leader in a business environment.

8. **Are you good at solving problems analytically?** Can you break a problem down to its components and attack each part individually in order to reach an overall solution?

Think of a problem you've been faced with, either professionally or personally, and recall the steps you took to resolve it. Managers are problem solvers. This is an attribute employers seek in any individual who's being groomed for advancement.

9. **Are you decisive?** Do you have the ability to make difficult decisions in a business environment that may affect others? Are you willing to take responsibility for those decisions? This is an extremely important trait for would-be managers.

Think of a time when you had to decide something that had an impact on other people in your life. What were the circumstances? Whether the result was positive or negative, recall how you handled it. How did the outcome affect you and the others involved? Did you take responsibility?

10. **Are you empathetic?** Can you view a situation from another person's perspective yet remain objective enough to offer sound reasoning and logic?

   If you have ever worked in customer service and handled complaints, or worked with children or the elderly, you probably had to exercise empathy in order to do your job well. It's a valuable skill that many lack, so emphasize it.

11. **Do you have good organizational and planning skills?** Can you manage your time effectively in order to maximize your productive potential?

   If you held down a job, took an average course load, got decent grades, and participated in extracurricular activities, then it's rather obvious that you have good time management skills. Be sure to point it out. Perhaps you held an office in your fraternity or sorority that required the ability to plan and organize fundraising events. That's another great way to prove your worth.

   Think hard. What in your past can you use as an example of your skills in this area?

12. **Are you detail-oriented?** An eye for detail is a strength when you can analyze the minor aspects of a project without losing sight of the overall result. It can be a weakness, however, if you're the type who gets hung up on and lost in the details.

   If you worked as a bank teller, an accounts receivable clerk, a proofreader, or even a cashier, chances are you can convince an employer you have an eye for detail. Remember, you should always try to draw from experiences beyond the classroom. You may have researched the world's most detailed term paper—we've all done that. Your time in the library doesn't cut the ice as an indicator of your attention to detail.

LOOKING AHEAD

Detail mania is a strength in many professions. A good accountant, for example, has to be concerned with every amount credited or debited but, to call it a strength, can never lose sight of the big picture—a set of perfectly balanced books.

13. **Do you have good management skills?** Do you have the ability to motivate others to higher achievement while still maintaining rapport and respect?

   The recruiters are looking for your potential. Even if your job title didn't involve management, perhaps something in your work history can convince an employer you'd make the grade as a manager. A lot of college students work in the lawn care business during the summer. Were you ever put in charge of a crew? If you were a lifeguard and promoted to senior lifeguard, that carries with it some management responsibilities. In any job, were you ever asked to assume responsibility for other staff members in the absence of management? Something as basic as being a team leader at McDonald's will work very nicely, too.

14. **Are you a people-oriented person?** Do you like coordinating your efforts on projects with others? Do you get along well in groups of people and with all types of people?

   People skills and communication skills are not the same thing. Someone can be an excellent orator and yet not have the ability to get along well with others.

   Talking about any job in which you dealt with the public is a good way of selling an employer on your people skills. If you've ever received a customer service award in a restaurant or retail job, say so. It's an excellent way of selling your ability to work well with a diverse group of people.

15. **Do you have quantitative and math skills?** Regardless of your degree, do you work well with numbers?

   Your grades in math and statistics classes are a good indication of your quantitative skills. If the job for which you're interviewing requires math aptitude, however, you shouldn't rely solely on your grades to sell your skills. A lot of my math-oriented clients volunteered as statisticians for their high school or college athletic teams. Quite a few have done temporary work for banks, as audit clerks, or doing checkbook reconciliation. Those tasks are good indicators of your quantitative skills. And if you have ever tutored in math or computer sciences, that's a noteworthy credential.

16. **Do you have good written communication skills?** Can you express your thoughts effectively on paper and relate information in an organized format that is easy for the reader to understand?

   Your cover letter and thank-you letter to the employer are real-life examples of your writing skills. In addition, many corporations give writing assignments as part of the interview process. Usually such tests mean that your writing skills will factor into your job performance.

Make every attempt to compose your letters clearly and concisely. Use good grammar and correct spelling, and always get someone else's opinion of your correspondence before mailing it to the employer.

Professional writers aren't the final editors or proofreaders of their own work. Follow their example and ask a literate friend to read your work with a fresh eye.

17. **Are you multitask-oriented?** Are you able to juggle several duties at once and see them all through to completion? Or are you the type who tackles only one assignment at a time?

Managers must be multitask-oriented. The ability to work on several projects simultaneously is a good selling point about yourself for a lot of different job descriptions. And someone who has the ability to "switch gears" easily from one assignment to the next shows excellent management potential.

Have you ever been asked to fill in for someone who was ill—someone whose duties were different from yours? Better yet, did you cover *both* jobs in the other person's absence? If any of your past employment required diversity of duties, the likelihood is you are able to thrive in a multitask job situation.

WAKE-UP CALL

In addition to the 17 strengths we've just covered, there are four others that employers find *most* appealing:

- a good work ethic
- the ability to learn quickly and easily
- self-motivation
- confident communication skills

Let me guess—you're not surprised. But the fact is that these skills are vital to employers, so vital that we'll examine them at length in the next chapter. For now, though, consider each one and start deciding where it fits in your inventory.

Part 2: What's your type?

The next step in your personal inventory is identifying your type. "Type" is an umbrella term that encompasses several factors. After evaluating your strengths, it's helpful to explore what sort of person you are in order to get the best career fit. People who enjoy psychology usually find this exercise especially fun.

YOUR PERSONAL INVENTORY, PART 2:
IDENTIFYING YOUR TYPE

1. **Are you a *generalist* or a *specialist*?** Can you do a lot of different types of job functions or do you specialize in a given area? A carpenter is a specialist. A teacher of carpentry is a generalist. An accountant is a specialist. A manager of accountants is a generalist.

2. **Are you *line-* or *staff*-oriented?** A line position relates directly to the reason the company exists. A baker in a bakery, a finisher in a manufacturing facility, or an accountant in an accounting firm are all employed in line functions.

   A staff position is any job within an organization that supports the line function. Some examples are: a secretary, an accountant in a manufacturing plant, or a quality control manager.

3. **Are you an *introvert* or an *extrovert*?** A person primarily interested in things outside the self, one who is outgoing, gregarious, and sociable, is an extrovert. An introvert is a self-contained person who is private and more introspective.

4. **Are you *active* or *passive*?** Are you the type of person who is a doer and one who generates action and activity? Or do you prefer to allow those around you and your surroundings to generate the activity?

5. **Are you more of a *technician*, an *administrator* or a *salesperson*?**

   Technicians are individuals who are scientifically, analytically, or mathematically inclined.

   Administrators possess good organizational and planning skills, set priorities in order of importance, and have good decision-making and problem-solving skills.

   Salespeople possess ego drive and empathy. They have the ability to sell themselves and their ideas convincingly and can generate enthusiasm in others.

6. **Do you thrive in a *structured* or an *unstructured* work environment?** Is your performance better when the rules are rigid, the majority of your work is performed from behind a desk, the work plan is laid out for you, and the job responsibilities are routine and predictable? The assembly line is almost a thing of the past, but there are still many careers that fit that description.

   Or, are you the type of individual who doesn't want to be glued to a desk? Do you perform better when you have freedom of movement and are responsible for designing your own work day?

Part 3: What are your weaknesses?

No personal inventory is complete without this step. It's very important to make yourself aware of your shortcomings in order to avoid job descriptions that would tax you in those areas.

This is a really tough exercise for most of my clients. Some are unable to come up with even one example of a weakness, and that's not good.

Maybe "weakness" is the wrong word, but it's a word that employers use often. So think of it this way: We're looking for pertinent *facts* about yourself. Not faults, misdeeds, or transgressions, just *facts* to help you screen in the right job possibilities and screen out the wrong ones.

YOUR PERSONAL INVENTORY, PART 3: ASSESSING YOUR WEAKNESSES

What's your greatest weakness?

Recruiters and interviewers think this is an important question. If you land a lot of interviews, I'm sure you'll hear it often.

Since we're all human and we all have weaknesses, it will work against you if you're unable to produce an example when this question arises. Interviewers are usually satisfied with one example, but you should always be prepared with at least two responses.

GOOD NEWS

The easiest method for identifying your weaknesses is to refer back to your list of strengths! Not many graduates can lay claim to the entire list.

Assessing your weaknesses, then, may be a simple process of elimination. Not everyone works well under pressure, is detail-oriented, has good writing skills, or works well in a team environment. Or maybe your weakness is the fact that you're computer-illiterate—a tough thing to admit these days.

Whichever weakness you pinpoint, prepare yourself to talk about it in interviews. Again, I promise you that the question will someday arise. You might think it will hurt you to talk about your negative qualities, but there's a trick to doing it that actually helps you instead.

If you're going to give the employer a negative quality about yourself, you don't want it to linger in the employer's memory. You must present it in a positive light. For example, you wouldn't say: "I think my greatest weakness is that I sometimes ramble on in conversations. I have a tendency to talk too much and say too little." Instead, you might say: "My greatest weakness is that I have a tendency to ramble. I sometimes talk too much and say too little. But I'm aware of the problem and have been working on my listening skills. Having become a better listener, I feel I'm becoming much more polished in my communication."

It's the old one-two punch. The key is always to think of the upside of your weakness. When presenting it to the employer, don't just drop the ball. Follow through. Let the interviewer know that you are improving in that area and are in the process of developing yet another strength.

Here are a few more examples.

Weakness: Lack of technical job skills, e.g., computers or software packages you haven't been exposed to.

Response: "I guess my greatest weakness is my lack of exposure to the software packages you use in this company. But I have the proven ability to pick things up very quickly and am confident I'd learn the system in a very short time." (This is a good place to insert a specific example.)

Weakness: Lack of exposure to working in a team-like environment.

Response: "I know I haven't had much experience working in a team-like environment, but I've taken the initiative to get involved in community service since graduating and am discovering I do pretty well working with groups of people."

Weakness: Poor writing skills.

Response: "I know my writing skills aren't the greatest, especially when it comes to spelling. I've been paying a lot of attention to it lately and am improving. In the process I'm developing an eye for detail I didn't know I had."

Now is the time to pinpoint your weaknesses because job-hunting gives you the initiative to improve them. If you lack leadership or management skills, take initiatives with your employer to land assignments requiring those skills in your job. If your communication skills aren't the greatest, join Toast Masters (a public speaking group) or take a Dale Carnegie course. If you're unable to manage your time effectively, read a book or two on the subject and start using a daily planner.

You get the idea and probably have a hundred better ideas. My point is that it is never too late to improve or to learn a new skill.

TRAPS TO AVOID

Here's my last tip on identifying your biggest weakness. Never use the old cliche: "I'm a perfectionist."

First of all, and most importantly, it's overused.

Second, half the population views perfectionism as a plus, not a minus. Your interviewer might consider it a great asset, for instance. You don't want to insult this person without realizing it!

Your personal inventory wasn't so bad, was it?

Okay, you can take a little breather now. You deserve it. Then try this career-smart exercise.

I suggest you sit down with a pen and paper and make a laundry list of your strengths and weaknesses. Carry them around with you for a few days. Talk about them with friends and family. Get some input from the people closest to you. If you're unable to come up with an experience to back up one of your strengths, maybe someone can provide insight or recall an experience you might have forgotten.

Once your inventory is complete, you can research job descriptions and confidently select one that matches your potential.

4

The Impression You Make

What Kind of Candidates Do Companies Hire?

"Forget this one! She comes across like a shark!"

Michelle had credentials you'd probably envy. Yet she may hold the record as one of my most difficult and hardest-to-place clients.

Her resume glowed in the dark. Michelle was a business management major from an Ivy League school with excellent grades, great internships and work history, superior communication skills, and a far above-average personal presentation and image.

Michelle was interested in account management opportunities and easily had the right stuff to succeed in the field. She succeeded in scheduling ten different interviews. Not one ended in an offer.

Feedback from the interviewers was basically the same. One manager praised Michelle's background but said there was no way he could hire her because she came across like a "shark." Another expressed concern that she would ruffle feathers among the people in his department. Another told me, only half-jokingly, that Michelle would probably go after her job in a year or so.

You get the picture. Although Michelle's credentials were well-received, Michelle wasn't.

People hire people. They don't hire Ivy League schools and high GPAs. Michelle was a star on paper and poison in person. She came across in the interviews as headstrong, aloof, arrogant, controlling, and cocky. She interviewed with a chip on her shoulder and as if the world owed her something. To put it mildly, her attitude and personality were standing in the way of an offer.

Realistically, I knew there was little hope of changing Michelle's personality at this point in her life. (And I knew that the right person to help with that project was a psychologist, not a career counselor.) What I could do for Michelle was to share employers' feedback with her, raise her awareness of how she was perceived, and encourage her to calm down a bit in future interviews.

As the saying goes, every pot has a lid. Michelle ultimately got and accepted an offer as a buyer for a major retailer in New York. That's a tough, fast-moving business in which many of Michelle's so-called negative qualities were viewed as positives.

Personality vs. performance

Employers recruit and interview candidates who have the education and basic skills to perform the duties of the job. But they *hire* the person who is the right *type*.

In an interview, the employer is evaluating much more than your ability to perform. Besides determining your suitability to the job description, employers look for other qualities—qualities that tell them what kind of person you are and indicate how well you might fit into their corporate culture.

The "Big Four" essentials

In Chapter 3 we covered 17 key qualities or strengths on which you need to assess yourself. You might recall that I also previewed four more strengths that employers look for (just before Part 2 of Your Personal Inventory). Now it's time to explore the Big Four in depth.

These four items are part of your self-evaluation checklist. But they outshine the others because they telegraph what *type* of person you have become.

Regardless of industry or job description, all organizations want their employees to possess these essentials. I've never known an organization that didn't value them. So you need to "sell" these universally sought strengths in every interview. It's actually an easy task if you fit the descriptions.

Essential #1: A strong work ethic

All employers want people who are willing to work hard. They look for those who will go the extra mile, seek out additional responsibilities, and work overtime if necessary.

How can you convince an employer of *your* strong work ethic? The following items work like a charm. Did you:

- Start working in junior high or high school, even if it was delivering newspapers or babysitting?
- Work during the school year?
- Seek out an internship or work without pay to get corporate exposure?
- Contribute to the payment of your education?
- Work steadily since securing your first job?
- Receive promotions or raises in past jobs based on your performance?

If you can answer "yes" to any of those questions, don't hesitate to blow your own horn. The phrase "work ethic" may sound old-fashioned but the concept is not.

Essential #2: The ability to learn quickly and easily

This one's a "must" for entry-level trainees. You'll be starting from scratch in a field where you are likely to have no experience. Employers are more confident in their decision to hire you if they feel you're a quick study. To find out if you fit this type, ask yourself:

- Have I ever been trained in another job—*any* job—and completed the training ahead of schedule or more quickly than previous employees?

- Have I ever done a job that offered no training, in which it was my responsibility to learn on my own with little or no supervision? How long did it take me to adapt to the position in comparison to other employees?
- Do I adapt easily to new business concepts, practices, and procedures? Can I prove it through past work experiences?

Essential #3: Confident communication skills

You say you've got the gift of gab? Your friends say you just love to hear yourself talk? Ah, but there are crucial differences between communication and *effective* communication.

Anyone can chat, answer questions, etc. But you're effective when you can express yourself verbally and be *clearly understood* by *just about anyone.*

Obviously, your verbal skills will be assessed in the actual interview. So you should speak clearly, enunciate, and use words in their proper context—that's extremely important. But you also have to let employers know that you can communicate well with different types of people and on different levels. Have you:

- Held jobs that involved customer service or sales?
- Worked at a company that required you to interact with different levels of management, co-workers, and customers alike?
- Held any telemarketing positions?
- Done any fundraising for your clubhouse or college alumni association or been active in community service?

Any of those situations allow you to sell yourself as someone who can communicate with people from all walks of life, socio-economic backgrounds, ages, and levels of intelligence. After all, if you're in telemarketing or customer service, you never know who's going to be on the other end of the phone or walking in the door next. It's been your job to deal with all of them effectively, whether you're peddling magazine subscriptions or dipping cones at Dairy Queen.

LOOKING AHEAD

Like sports or entertainment, the business world has its own language and shorthand. Immerse yourself in it by browsing through the business section of the newspaper, reading business periodicals (e.g., *BusinessWeek, The Wall Street Journal, Fortune, Forbes*), and tuning in to business news on TV and radio. Try to keep abreast of what's happening in corporate life. You will be better versed and more fluent in conversations with potential employers if you have an idea of what the economy and the financial market are doing.

Essential #4: Are you a self-starter?

What's the difference between being motivated and *self*-motivated? About a world of difference, I have observed.

Employers want individuals who can motivate themselves to get the job done, who don't need outside prompting to take the initiative to tackle the next assignment. They covet candidates who possess the drive to complete their training in order to be able to work independently and be 100 percent productive.

Selling the employer on the fact that you're a self-starter can be easily accomplished if you:

- Took an internship with no pay to get the exposure you needed.
- Held down a job even though your education was being paid for by your family or through a trust fund or scholarship.
- Started and ran your own business over summer breaks, e.g., lawn services, messenger or delivery services, or even babysitting.

More about self-motivation. I want to spend a little extra time on the benefits of being self-motivated.

"Okay, okay," you may be saying. "I get the point."

But a lot of my clients really *don't* get the point. It's extremely valuable to understand *why* employers like self-starters so very much and view motivation as one of the four essentials.

Sure, it's obvious that a high level of motivation is essential for would-be trainees being groomed for management. Employers want to know exactly what price you are willing to pay in order to get where you want to go with your career.

Are you willing to relocate? To wait two or three years for your first major promotion? To work long hours? To make sacrifices for your career? Your responses are very clear indicators of whether or not you're management material.

But another reason employers love to recruit self-starters is not as apparent: It has to do with money.

The bucks start here. Training programs are an expensive undertaking for a corporation. A year of your training can cost as much as $20,000, *not* including your salary. For each week of classroom education provided by the company, the bill can top $1,500. And that's a very modest estimate.

Expenses add up fast when they include travel, hotels, meals, the salaries of your trainers, and more. Then there's the money-draining fact that, until you learn the job and are making a contribution to the company, a portion of your salary is considered overhead. You are not yet producing as you should, and your income isn't fully justified until you do.

Most corporations set up their training programs on a self-motivational basis and the programs are designed for an average person to succeed. You'll get some classroom education and lots of on-the-job training. In many cases you'll be given books and manuals to study both at home and at work. You'll be evaluated frequently as you progress through the training materials, and in many cases, you'll be tested at certain points along the way.

These programs are designed this way in order to allow maximum
benefit to the trainee and the company. Not everyone learns or absorbs
information at the same rate and speed. A motivated person will be
likely to complete training ahead of schedule, thereby saving the company money. Quick learners also avoid the boredom that might accom-
pany a more rigid training schedule. They also achieve self-satisfaction
and increase their self-esteem as they mark their progress through
training. Everyone's a winner!

Tonya's story. *To employers, self-motivated candidates are some of
the most highly desirable recruits. Tonya is a perfect example. She
graduated from a state university with a general business degree. She
took six years to graduate. She changed her major four or five times and
took classes every summer she was in college. Her overall GPA was a
2.1. Certainly, her credentials were not the best.*

*On the up side, Tonya was extremely personable. Plainly and sim-
ply, I just* liked *her. In addition, I had a great deal of respect for her
work ethic and motivation. She worked forty hours a week waiting on
tables the entire time she was in school and paid 100 percent of her education and living expenses.*

*When Tonya came to me, she oozed motivation. She made mistakes
in her college career and was now prepared to pay the price. She had a
willingness to start anywhere, doing anything, if I could just get her in
the door of a major corporation.*

*After counseling Tonya, I sent her on her first interview with a
major telecommunications company in Chicago for a position in customer service. She had the personality, the required BS degree, and the
communication skills necessary to succeed in the job. The employer
loved her attitude and drive and extended her an offer. Tonya got her
wish … an entry-level career with a Fortune 100 company.*

*That was nearly six years ago. Today, Tonya has a master's degree
from DePaul University—of course, her employer footed the bill—and a
position of much greater responsibility within the organization. Her career is on track and I doubt she'll ever wait on tables again (unless she
wants to). I attribute Tonya's success to her self-motivation. And, yes, to
her likability.*

An equation you didn't learn in algebra class.   My final thought
on motivation is a very simple equation for you to consider. It's worth
posting alongside other nuggets you've gathered along the way:

The constant in the equation is the ability. Nearly every college graduate has the ability. But the variable—the level of motivation—is what will ultimately determine the degree of success you'll experience in your job search and your career.

I hope you have a deeper understanding of why employers universally seek the Four Essentials. If you can call these qualities your own, sell them in each and every interview. Don't worry about sounding like every other job candidate out there. You won't.

Additional essentials

Surprise! Here are five more essential points to ponder. This set is tricky. They're not as easily sold as the Four Essentials. What's more, in these areas you're evaluated not so much by *what* you say, but by *how* you say it.

Essential #5: The right attitude

How much of yourself are you willing to invest in order to get what you want? Your employment history might tell the recruiter about your work ethic, but it doesn't give any indication of your *attitude* about work. The way you answer the employer's questions telegraphs your attitude loud and clear.

In a salaried position, and in management in particular, you must stay at work until the job is done. If the issue of long hours arises in the interview, and you immediately ask about overtime compensation or how often people have to put in long days, you convey a negative attitude. At best, you're sending this unspoken message: "Sure, I'll work hard, but what's in it for me?" Not good.

During the first interview, *never* bring up salary, benefits, company perks, vacations, and sick day policies unless the interviewer does. You'll have plenty of time to learn everything you need to learn in your second or third interview.

WAKE-UP CALL

To paraphrase John F. Kennedy: *Ask not what your company can do for you. Ask what you can do for your company.*

If you get the job, your company *will* do a lot for you. A good employment relationship is a two-way street. But at the interview, be prepared to do all the giving and none of the taking.

Drop the negativity. In every interview, your past employment will definitely be a topic of conversation. Keep in mind that where you worked is sometimes not as important as what you did or how you did it.

The golden rule is: *You cannot display a negative attitude toward any previous employer, manager, or job.* Even when you've had a boss from hell (and we all have), or worked under less-than-desirable conditions, always draw on the positive. What have you learned from the experience and how has it contributed to your growth and maturity?

When I ask my clients about previous employers and why they left their jobs, I frequently hear the following:

- "My boss was disorganized and never knew what he was doing."
- "My manager always took credit for things that I and other coworkers had done."
- "My boss and I just didn't see eye to eye."

Any of those responses in an interview will most likely be a strike against you and, potentially, a reason to keep you out of the running.

I'm not asking you to be hypocritical. In the first example, for instance, you need not tell the interviewer your *boss* was disorganized. Instead, you can say the *work environment* was *sometimes* chaotic and disorganized, but it helped you learn how to organize and manage your time more effectively.

DAMAGE CONTROL

It always works in your favor to take a negative situation and cast a positive light on it. That's the only attitude an employer really wants to see.

Job outlook vs. career outlook. Employers want to know you're aware of the difference between a job and a career. You probably know the difference already, but it's worth a brief review.

A job is something you do every day, day in and day out. Your job description remains basically the same from week to week, month to month, year to year. If you have worked at the Walnut Stamping Plant on the production line for 22 years, your job description has probably changed very little in that time.

In a career, however, your job description changes as you grow within the company. With each promotion, you assume new responsibilities and outgrow and/or delegate some of your work to others. Careers change, grow, and evolve, as do the people in them.

If you ask an employer where you can expect to find yourself in management three to five years down the line, you send the message that you're career-oriented. You're indicating a willingness to work hard

LOOKING AHEAD

A willingness to relocate is another excellent sign of a career-minded individual. In fact, being *un*willing to relocate is likely to turn a career back into a job.

A relocation usually means a promotion and a change in job description. If you turn down the promotion because you don't want to move, you will most likely remain in the same position with the same job description. When the growth stops, the career ends and the job starts!

and invest yourself in the company in order to advance. Letting the employer know you're the type of person who takes on additional responsibilities outside of your job description without being asked is another way of telegraphing that you have a good attitude about your career.

Essential #6: The right personality

When it comes to personality, there is no right or wrong. All the same, your personality is a key consideration in an interview. As I said before: People hire people, they don't hire degrees and GPAs.

When extending a job offer to one of my candidates, employers often say something like this: "It was a tough choice, but we decided on Terry because she seemed to click with everyone in the department."

Every corporation has a personality, or a corporate culture, and every division and department within it also has a personality. A department manager must take into consideration whether a new hire is likely to fit in.

A zebra can't change its stripes, and obviously you can't transform yourself into someone you're not. But there is a way to deal with this fact of life. Here it is:

> *The wisest thing you can do for yourself in an interview*
> *is to be yourself.*
> *Conversely, one of the biggest mistakes you can make*
> *is* not *to be yourself.*

Michelle was an exception to this rule. In her case, being herself meant being abrasive. If you are the type who is normally overly confident, cocky, and headstrong, your personality can overwhelm an interviewer. My advice is to eat a piece of humble pie before you go to the interview. The company has something you want and you'll never get it if you're impertinent and demanding. Being gracious, cordial, courteous, and pleasant will go a long way in toning down an overbearing personality.

Don't become a "suit." Many college graduates think it's to their benefit to adopt an "interviewing personality." When they put on that navy-blue interviewing suit, suddenly they become different people. They start behaving and talking as they *think* they should, instead of in their usual way.

Of course you should prepare for every interview and always put your best foot forward. If your usual behavior includes belching or cursing or trashing people, do *not* put it on display. (And expect to wait about forty years for your first job offer.) But never try to be someone you're not, because then no one will be able to figure out where you fit in.

TRAPS TO AVOID

Some people think they'll be perceived as more professional if they use big words and phrases in an interview. I'm talking about words you wouldn't normally use in daily conversation. Example: "I accrued much experience as a fast-food cashier and, despite the frenzied environment, found it a transformational involvement in terms of my burgeoning professional development."

A giant mistake!

However well-meaning, language like this makes you sound stiff and phony to the employer. And it's been my experience that people frequently use such words out of context, making them sound, in a word, ridiculous.

Too cool is uncool. Along the same vein, many candidates think they shouldn't get excited in interviews. But by trying to stay cool, they risk coming across as blasé.

It is *not* unprofessional to show enthusiasm in an interview. Don't stifle it; let it work for you. Employers love candidates who are eager about their company and the job opportunity at hand. If you're enthusiastic about what they're saying in the interview, let it show.

One other factor that transforms personalities for the worse is fear. Don't blow the interview out of proportion. Regard it as just a conversation, which it is. If you are fearful and tense, it will show not only in your answers but in your posture. Relax. Be yourself!

Essential #7: The right aptitudes

Aptitudes are skills and abilities that can be measured against other relative levels. Your aptitudes are either inborn or acquired through practice, training, and conditioning.

One person can sit at a piano at age six and play a flawless concerto. Another can play the same concerto, but only after 12 years of piano lessons. Both have musical aptitude, but one was virtually born with it while the other had to develop it.

Nobody expects you to be a natural genius, but nobody knows of your special skills either—unless you tell them. Figure out how your abilities relate to your potential job and employer, then talk them up in the interview.

Computer skills are a good example. Most business colleges require one or two basic computer classes, usually taken during freshman year. Recruiters know this. They'll assume these classes are the sum and substance of your computer knowledge, which translates into limited high-tech exposure and little working knowledge of any programs. (This obviously doesn't apply to computer science majors.) Your perceived lack of computer literacy may then screen you out of contention at many companies.

But maybe your college had computer-integrated classrooms. Maybe you've worked on a PC since you were in grade school and can write programs blindfolded. The employer will assume your computer knowledge is equivalent to that of every other graduate with a business degree *unless you point out your special aptitude.*

Essential #8: The right potential

Because you are being considered for an entry-level position, a primary concern for employers is your development potential. They are going to evaluate your skills and abilities and determine if you have potential for advancement if given the proper training and conditioning. In essence, they are looking for your potential strengths.

Training programs are designed to draw on those potential strengths. The company will provide the necessary education to help develop your potential into a useful, significant skill.

Employers usually evaluate your development potential based on previous employment. If you worked for the same company over three consecutive summers and each year your job responsibilities increased, it shows you have the developmental skills they're looking for. If you had an internship and the company extended your stay or gave you additional responsibility, it indicates you will likely show the same kind of development in the training program.

Essential #9: The right character

Your character traits are the intangibles that reflect your personal code of ethics. Honesty, integrity, trustworthiness, dependability, and generosity are just a few examples.

In fact, making an issue of your character traits in an interview sometimes causes the employer to question what you say. Remember the line from *Macbeth*: "The lady doth protest too much."

Let's take honesty as an example. During an interview, I assume that if I leave my office for a phone call, nothing will be missing from my desk when I return. When I have clients who mention repeatedly how honest and trustworthy they are, I begin to wonder why they're hammering home the point. My natural reaction is to doubt their honesty. (And to double-check my desk for loss of pilfered pens.)

There's another angle to consider as well. A common interview request is: "Tell me your greatest strengths." I do this a little differently;

I ask candidates to give me three words or phrases which best describe them, because I think that approach is a little less intimidating. But the basic premise is the same.

Invariably, nine out of ten people put "honesty" at the top of their lists. Don't be one of them. Any other answer you give will set you apart from your competition. When asked in an interview what your greatest strength is, or how you'd describe yourself, use the question as an opportunity to sell a strength, not a character trait (and especially *not* honesty!).

Covering all the bases.   With the exception of character traits, you should make every attempt in each of your interviews to address all of the issues I've covered in this chapter. Otherwise you'll run the risk of allowing employers to draw their own conclusions about your attitudes or experiences. Chances are those conclusions will be negative.

Remember, employers are conditioned to screen people out, to consign as many as possible as quickly as possible to the scrap heap. Upon receiving 300 resumes in response to an ad, the first thing an employer does is to look for reasons to toss 290 of them. In interviewing situations, the numbers are smaller but the principle is identical. Down to ten candidates? Let's look for reasons to cut seven. With the field down to three, the final task is to screen out two.

Now that you realize the dynamics of this draft pick, don't give employers any reason to eliminate you. In the early stage of reviewing resumes, they may toss you aside for something as seemingly inconsequential as a misspelled word or a missing phone number. In the interviewing stage, you may be rejected because you didn't cover all your bases.

Know the job description and know what type of person the employer is looking for. Then deliver it, without attitude, in the interview—gift-wrapped in your navy-blue suit.

5

Zero In on Your Job Market

Packaging and Presenting

"20 interviews and one crummy offer"

In my first interview with anyone, I always ask how many job interviews they've had. When Joe answered "Twenty," I was quite surprised by it. Joe himself was depressed by it.

"Feel good about your twenty interviews," I quickly told him. "It's not easy landing even one. Most of my clients have had fewer than five interviews by the time they come to me." Joe visibly perked up.

Information on previous interviews is very important to me as a counselor and recruiter. First and most obviously, it eliminates duplication of effort if you've already interviewed with one of my client companies. But it also clues me in to your level of motivation, your possible career path, your knowledge of the job market, and your interviewing skills.

I asked Joe how many of his interviews resulted in callbacks or offers. Now this was depressing. He had gotten exactly one offer, following a 30-minute interview, for a job in commission-only, door-to-door sales.

At this point I suspected one of two problems. Either Joe's interviewing skills were very poor, or he had been interviewing for the wrong jobs.

For Joe, the latter was the case. He was looking in all the wrong places and, not surprisingly, finding all the wrong kinds of careers.

In most of Joe's interviews, he knew nothing about the company or position prior to showing up. Once there, he discovered the majority of jobs were sales-related or required experience he didn't have. Joe was not the sales type. He also didn't understand his job market very well or even know where to find it.

Being somewhat clueless, Joe had spent too much time spinning his wheels and wasting his time. He had nothing to show for his efforts except discouragement and rejection letters. I assured him that the interviewing experiences were valuable in themselves, but we had a lot of work to do.

With all my talk about work ethic and the like, you might be surprised to know that I've always been a big believer in taking the path of least resistance. (The two concepts are not mutually exclusive.)

Interviewing and landing an offer doesn't have to be an uphill battle. If you understand marketing—if you know what your market is and know where to find it—the business of landing your first career job becomes less frustrating.

Defined in advertising terms, marketing is the preparation of a product for the marketplace. If Procter & Gamble develops a new product, the next step is to determine how to market it in order to make it stand out on the grocery store shelf and make you want to buy it.

How much should it cost? Where should the product be positioned to generate the most sales? What price is the competition charging for a similar product and how does it compare? What kind and color of packaging should be used? What should the package copy say about the product? What benefits does this product have over the competition and how do we communicate that to the consumer?

In your case, *you* are the product. The entry-level job market is your marketplace and the employer is going to be doing the buying. Your competition in the marketplace is your fellow graduates, all looking for their first career positions.

Think of yourself as a new detergent or a hot new type of nacho chip—whatever sort of product turns you on. Then ask yourself some of the same questions we asked about Procter & Gamble's new product. How much are you worth in the marketplace? What target market will generate the most interest in what you have to offer? What salary is your competition pulling in? What's your image like and how might it be improved? What do you want to say about yourself in the interview that will help distinguish you from those who interview before and after you? What do you have to offer the prospective employer that your competitors do not?

LOOKING AHEAD

Approaching your career search from the product/market angle will help you develop a better understanding of the job market, your competition, yourself, and exactly where you fit in.

In previous chapters we did a lot of work on developing a better understanding of yourself. Now it's time to look outward.

The phantom marketplace

The job market is always there. Just open the newspaper to the want ad section and behold column upon column of jobs, seemingly there for the taking.

But are they the jobs you want? Are you qualified? Do you have the experience? Are they in the field you're pursuing? For recent college graduates, the answers are usually no, no, no.

One of the first things you have to do is define your market. Having a four-year degree with no experience makes you a "unique" product. Even if you've been out of college for two years and have held a job, or a series of nonprofessional jobs, you are still viewed by an employer as an inexperienced candidate, which puts you in that unique category.

When the product is unique, you have to find a niche market in which to sell it. In these cases, the most likely niche would be the entry-level market. In my opinion, entry-level training programs are *the key market* for a young professional with no related corporate experience. Sure, there are other opportunities out there for a college graduate trying to land a first career position but, remember, we're going for the path of least resistance.

Basic training (and I don't mean the military)

What kind of companies offer training programs and are in the market for a recent college grad with no experience? And where do you find them? The answer: Major corporations, to be found anywhere in the United States where the corporation has a branch with training capabilities.

Companies in the market for trainees are often Fortune 500 companies, because they have resources that small to medium-size companies usually don't have. Entry-level training programs cost employers about $20,000 per year, per trainee. Some programs—like many of the ones I represent—run for up to two years. The final bill is $40,000 for one trainee, not including salary and benefits!

Smaller companies simply can't afford the luxury of hiring a trainee. Sure, they may hire entry-level candidates, but your training will be brief and strictly on-the-job. People with experience may also be competing for these positions. And smaller companies are likely to choose the candidate who can hit the ground running.

WAKE-UP CALL

In searching for training programs, also note the following: If the corporation is in a service-oriented industry, it's usually decentralized. That means it has a corporate headquarters, regional offices, and branches located nationwide and sometimes worldwide. These branches are usually equipped to hire their trainees through independent recruiting as opposed to having recruits supplied through corporate headquarters.

Starting your career in companies like these is a great way to increase your opportunities for advancement. The more branches your employer has, the more management positions they have for you to grow into, especially if you're willing to relocate. (There's that magic word again. More about it soon.)

So where do you find the good programs? Start with the Fortune 500. Take a trip to the library. Do some homework and you'll soon discover that these companies are scattered throughout the United States, with a higher concentration in the Midwest, the Mid-Atlantic states, the Northeast Corridor, and the West Coast.

Campus interviews: When your market comes to you

By all means, start your career search among those companies that visit your campus. They are there to interview because they hire entry-level candidates—usually. It will be the first and *only* time your market comes to you.

But you may find slim pickings. The size and reputation of your college or university determines the quality and quantity of the recruiters you're likely to see. A small liberal arts college nestled in the rolling hills of the Ohio Valley will attract fewer companies, and fewer big names, than Carnegie Mellon, the University of Southern California, Purdue, or The Ohio State University.

Furthermore, the companies visiting your campus usually have a corporate office nearby. Generally speaking, the only time a corporation will send a recruiter to campuses outside its geographic boundaries is to locate a specific kind of candidate, such as engineers. Then, they'll focus on the country's top engineering schools.

One trip to your college recruitment office will probably alert you not to put all your eggs in this flimsy basket. The percentage of college seniors placed through on-campus interviews is very low, only about 5 percent on average.

Make the trip, however, and get out of it whatever you can. The staffers at your college recruiting office are a good resource. Use them, but don't expect them to do all the work and don't expect them to have all the answers. The placement office is merely your first stop in your journey to your first career job.

Empty opportunities and bogus visits

Just because a company comes on campus to interview, don't assume that they have great things to offer. Many placement offices, frankly, aren't too particular about their on-campus roster. They have to justify their existence, so they may accept all takers.

Usually, your school's proximity to a metropolitan area is in direct proportion to the number of quality campus interviews you can expect. In more remote locations, at best you might be visited by small, local companies that offer very little training and dismal growth potential. Slightly bigger companies might say they're looking for "management trainees." In the interview you discover they're looking for people to sell life insurance. (That's an extremely tough field to succeed in as a raw trainee!)

Another disappointment, which happens all too often, is that you learn during an on-campus interview that the employer doesn't have any openings. They're making an appearance as a favor to the school

DAMAGE CONTROL

Here's an inside tidbit that might change your attitude about "no jobs right now" interviews.

I've seen many companies *create* openings for exceptional candidates. In some circumstances, the company will play with its budget to hire Sally Gold-Star in June, and then hire one less trainee that September. I've also had corporations extend offers to my clients with a start date six months after the interview. They do this either to remain within their recruiting budgets, or because company policy is to conduct only one or two training programs a year with all the recruits sharing the same start date.

So when you hear those words "we're screening for the future," hang in instead of tuning out.

or the alumni association. Their line is: "We have no present needs but are screening for future openings."

Upsetting? Yes, of course. Most college grads tell me they give up in the interview upon hearing that news. Worse yet, I detect, they assume a less-than-positive attitude. If you find yourself in this admittedly annoying situation, that's still probably the worst thing you can do.

By now, you're wise to all the good reasons to treat every interview as if it matters. Don't develop a "what's the use" attitude—interviewers can sense it.

My advice, all in all, is to secure as many campus interviews as possible. Do your research, learn about the company and position, and then interview to the best of your ability. In my opinion, it's better to interview well enough to get a mediocre offer and turn it down than not to get an offer at all.

Even if you don't land an offer on campus, you're gaining knowledge about the job market and practicing your interviewing skills. It's batting practice.

The black hole: Newspaper want ads

If you're one of the 95 percent who didn't get lucky finding a job on campus, exactly how do you turn up a trainee spot? One thing is certain: *The newspaper want ads are not the answer.* You saw what they did for poor Joe.

The best career opportunities for first-time job seekers usually never make the classifieds. Corporations find it more cost-effective and convenient to recruit their trainees on college campuses or through select recruiting services. Why spend money on newspaper ads (they *are* expensive)—and then sift through hundreds of resumes, faxes, and phone calls—when you can have the right candidates hand-delivered to you?

More black holes: Employment agencies

So, you may be thinking, how about employment agencies? Isn't it their job to find jobs for people like me?

Sorry to be the bearer of so much bad news, but don't expect to have much luck at employment agencies, either. They're generally in the business of finding experienced people to fill jobs requiring experience and specific skill sets.

Employment agencies work for employers, not for you. Employers pay them for the service of recruiting experienced candidates. Typical agency fees are usually 1 percent per thousand dollars of first year's earnings, with a ceiling of 25 to 30 percent. Do the math. At 25 percent, a company would have to pay agencies $6,250 to hire a $25,000-

a-year trainee. On top of that, they would also have to absorb the pense of training.

That's a lot of money to invest in someone who has no prov track record, which is why companies don't take the gamble. There are other, cheaper ways to recruit entry-level candidates.

Additionally, most employment agencies recruit and place people in their own backyards. They advertise local openings and recruit local people to fill them. If you're open to relocation, as you should be, you're limiting yourself when you rely on a local employment agency to find a job for you.

Entry-level search firms: Now you're getting hot!

If you are fortunate enough to have access to search firms that deal in the trainee market, absolutely take advantage of their services. They'll be able to get you into interviews much more easily than you yourself can. They have the contacts, know the companies and the types of candidates they recruit, and can accomplish in days what it may take you months to do independently.

Don't forget, searching for a career is a job in itself. If you knew of a tool to help you get the job done more easily, wouldn't you use it? Entry-level search firms are specialists in the recruitment field, so it might take a little effort to find one. Ultimately, it will be worth the effort.

If you work with a search firm of this nature, there most likely will be a fee for the recruiter's service. Corporations are usually unwilling to pick up the tab.

Earlier, I explained how employment agencies determine their fees. Now, I think it's important for you to understand why a corporation doesn't *have* to or *want* to pay a fee for a trainee.

Major companies have at least one salaried recruiter in the human resource department. This person is being paid to visit campuses and select the best qualified graduates. They don't have to pay the campus to hire the graduate, so why would they pay a recruiter to hire you?

A corporation also considers a trainee a "high risk" employee. After all, the company is bringing you on board with *no* experience. Their decision to hire you was based on your potential. What if they were wrong?

Companies invest lots of money in trainees, as you know. They are not willing to increase their risk by paying a service charge to hire you and then discover nine months from now that you're not cut out for the position.

So corporations will pay fees to hire an experienced person, if they must. They're getting what they're paying for: someone to walk in and take over the job without much downtime, training expense, or risk of failure. Otherwise, *they have access to all the "free" entry-level candidates they want.*

If paying a fee to a specialized search firm feels like a waste of your money, consider the pluses.

Generally, a recruiter specializing in entry-level searches can help you find a good job faster than you can do it on your own. Remember how most of my clients are placed within six weeks?

Your unassisted job search will take nine months, on average. If a recruiter can place you in one month, I guarantee your fee will be only a fraction of the eight months of lost income you experienced while you looked on your own.

What's more, if you go to work for a corporation with a tuition refund program, your recruiter's fee is like payment in advance for your master's degree. I assure you that this fee will be far less than the price of two years of graduate school.

Before using any search firm, I suggest you check their references carefully and learn exactly how they operate before signing on the dotted line. Many clients ask me for references and I always gladly oblige. I'm happy to have them contact the people I've successfully placed. Other would-be clients sometimes ask for the names of the companies I work with.

WAKE-UP CALL

Reputable recruiters are happy to refer potential clients to past customers. However, we won't share the names of companies who are currently hiring through us—until we get a commitment from you about using our services.

By sharing such information, we'd run the risk of having you contact the company directly. And that would threaten our livelihood.

Firms and scams to avoid

Think twice about a recruiting firm that charges anything up front.

Most reputable recruiters work on a contingency basis. You'll have nothing to lose if the recruiter can't deliver a job. If someone demands money at the outset, I'd definitely keep on looking. In fact, if you have any doubt at all about the search firm and the way it presents its services, call the Better Business Bureau in your community. Shoddy firms tarnish the overall industry and cheat innocent job-seekers along the way.

There's one other type of employment "service" I'd like to warn you about. For a set fee, usually several hundred dollars, they offer you a "professionally done resume" and a marketing "service," which usually amounts to a list of companies and addresses in industries in which you've expressed an interest. Usually, such services don't even mail your resume to these companies. You, old chump, do the work and pay the postage.

The listed companies may or may not have openings; the employment service doesn't care. They make their money from selling you a mailing list and a rewritten resume.

In fact, blind mailings are very ineffective whether you do them from scratch or hire a bogus "service" to help. In my entire recruiting career, I have never met a recent college graduate who secured a good interview through this method. If you want to try this type of marketing, however, begin by going to the library or your college placement office. The same information provided to you by this type of bogus employment service can be found in those places free of charge.

Relocation: Taking the product to the marketplace

The last and most important advice I can give you on locating your marketplace is to open yourself up to the possibility of relocation.

I know: You hate the very idea. It's a knee-jerk reaction that deserves to be deconstructed.

Don't forget that you're a unique product looking for a career in a limited job market. That means you have to take the product *to* the marketplace. And that might mean relocation.

When you examine the benefits of relocation, you'll probably drop your resistance. So let's discuss some of the pros and cons of being relocatable.

Good reasons to relocate

Consider this: You are more relocatable now than you'll ever be again. If you're a typical recent grad, you're probably between 21 and 25 years old, have no career tying you down, no spouse, no children, and no mortgage. You probably have very little in the way of furniture and personal belongings, making moving uncomplicated. Okay, you may be tied into a lease, but check the laws in your state. Renter's rights are usually protected. If your employment requires you to move out of your area, most leases can be broken.

Another tremendous benefit of relocation is that it will dramatically increase your market in the number of opportunities available. Think of how many major corporations hire entry-level trainees in your city. Next, think of how many major market cities are within a five- or six-hour drive of where you live. In most cases that should cover the state in which you live. Now multiply the number of major cities by the number of opportunities in your hometown. It's really very simple. The more you broaden your geographic boundaries, the greater your odds are of securing an interview, at the very least.

Being open to relocation will also expose you to more kinds of training programs in a wider variety of industries. This is particularly im-

portant if you hold a degree in chemical engineering, marine biology, graphic design, or other specialties. Relocation will increase the chances for you to secure employment in a field directly related to your education.

In short, I firmly believe that relocation is the key to upward mobility. Fortune 500s recruit candidates who are willing to relocate. And then there are all those service-oriented corporations which tend to be decentralized. Each branch has its own management structure, which translates into more growth opportunities for those who are willing to move.

Relocation is crucial, in fact, if you join a Fortune 500 training program and stay within the organization. Then you should anticipate two to three moves in ten years. This is not always the case—the days when IBM stood for "I've Been Moved" are largely over—but usually applies. It only stands to reason that if a company is spending big money to groom you for management, it's going to want someone who's willing to move to get there.

Here's a delightful point to ponder: A willingness to relocate to a larger market often means a higher starting salary. The smaller the city and the company, by contrast, the smaller your initial paychecks.

Job offers tend to come faster when you are willing to expand your interviewing horizons. That's why *all* of my clients are relocatable— even if they didn't think so when they first walked in my door. They're the nucleus of the group that lands great offers within four to six weeks.

As you realize all too well by now, most graduates take nine to twelve months to find an entry-level position, even in a good economy. What stretches out the time frame is that most grads don't even consider the possibility of relocation, at least until they have reached a point of desperation and have exhausted all of their local options.

Reasons not to relocate (but I'll try to convince you otherwise)

Trot out your strongest protests against relocating, and I'll match you point for point. I've heard all the objections and I just don't buy them.

It's true that relocation will move you away from family, friends, and a familiar environment. But if your relationships are strong and solid, they will remain so regardless of where you might choose to live.

If breaking away seems difficult, remember that you can return home on weekends and holidays, call home frequently, exchange letters and e-mail, and invite your family for visits. As for friends, I guarantee it won't be long until you establish a new social circle. And you'll still have the gang you left back home.

Besides, relocation need not be forever. Once you've been trained and have a few years of experience under your belt, you can always request a transfer to an office closer to your hometown. A smart employer would rather move you than lose you.

Another option after having gained a few years of experience is to return to your hometown and market yourself to other companies. It's much easier to secure your second good job after having been trained by a major corporation. You're transformed into a much more marketable candidate.

In short, I just can't think of any truly compelling reason why a recent college graduate would choose not to relocate if it means the difference between a career and a job, or between a job and no job at all.

Dealing with competition in the marketplace

So far we've talked in depth about understanding yourself and scoping out what employers are looking for. Now, what about your competition?

When Procter & Gamble launches a new product into the marketplace, you can be assured they have thoroughly researched similar products offered by their competitors. You must do the same.

Your competition is every other person with a minimum four-year degree who's looking for a first career position. That makes the entry-level job market one of the toughest. The problem isn't just the sheer number of candidates, but the similarities of the competition.

On the surface, you and your competition have more likenesses than distinctions. You all have four-year degrees, a major, and no related experience. You all have a GPA and extracurriculars. You all took

GOOD NEWS

You're part of a huge mass of people chasing what seems like a diminishing number of career positions. But don't lose too much sleep over the fact. Every generation has had its hard times, but people have always survived and forged decent careers. Don't fall prey to the idea that you missed the "golden age" of careers. Golden ages are myths. In 20 years, people will be looking back at *this* era as a golden age.

basically the same classes, working on case studies and research projects. You're all between the ages of about 21 and 25 years old, are almost always single, and most of you have work histories that look like patchwork quilts.

So we're back to credentials—everything in your background that can be documented. The school you attended, your grade point average, the type of degree, your age and involvement in extracurriculars can all be looked up and verified by a recruiter. When you send out a resume, you're presenting your credentials to the employer.

If you planned your college career effectively and have above-average credentials, you're already a step ahead of your competition. But while a well-presented set of credentials (see Chapters 7 and 8 on resumes) might get you through the interviewing door, they won't tell the employer who you are as a person and they won't necessarily land you an offer.

Since you and most of your competitors have similar credentials, you can't rely on them to set you apart. In interviews, your credentials won't be of much value at all. In fact, whatever position you're interviewing for, the recruiter probably selected potential candidates with very similar credentials based on the opening the company is trying to fill.

Okay, maybe you graduated in less than four years or completed your master's degree in one year. Congratulations, for real! Getting your degree *was* an achievement that sets you apart from your competition.

Pull out your Personal Inventory and take another, harder look at yourself. That's where Joe and countless others had to begin. What other goals have you set and achieved that distinguish you from the competition?

Did you meet your objective to pass a double major? Speak two languages? Study abroad? Pay for your own education? Start your own

TRAPS TO AVOID

Most recent graduates spend too much precious time during interviews trying to sell the employer on their credentials. They talk about their classes, case studies, grades, fraternities, and the like. They don't look any deeper or think beyond the limits of their education.

Let me illustrate. Like many recruiters, I always ask my clients to tell me "a goal you've set for yourself and achieved." Nine times out of ten, the answer is related to the fact that they got their degree.

Well, I think to myself, so did the people who interviewed before and after them! Remember, the company is recruiting only *degreed* candidates!

The moral of the story is not to sound like a clone. Read on.

lawn service company or babysitting service? Did you hold a job where setting goals or meeting quotas was part of the drill?

In the interview, your most saleable assets are those drawn from your Personal Inventory. They are the skills and abilities you've developed as a result of securing your credentials and, in general, living your life. All of your competition went to college and got a degree, but each of you developed distinct skills to varying degrees in the process.

Having completed your Personal Inventory, you will be much better prepared to face your competition. The better you know your product, the better you'll be able to set yourself apart from your competition and sell yourself to the employer in the interview.

6

Networking

Making Connections at the Entry Level

If my clients had been successful at the business of networking, they wouldn't have been my clients at all. They wouldn't have needed my help.

Networking to land interviews works best after you have a few years of experience under your belt. That's not to say it can't be effective at the entry level; it just has to be done a little differently.

People who have been employed in a professional capacity for five years have learned who their competitors are and what kinds of industries are interested in their experience. They've also made professional connections by attending seminars and conventions, participating in professional organizations, and pursuing certification in their fields. Most of this simply isn't applicable to someone a year or two out of college.

But don't despair. By the end of this chapter you'll have some solid new ideas for networking, even if your social and professional circles feel quite limited right now.

It's all about building a base.

In trying to network for your first career job, you have to know where to look and what to look for *before* you try to pull strings to get your foot in the door.

Without benefit of job experience or corporate exposure, your first assignment is to build a networking base by researching industries and companies that offer the positions you're interested in pursuing. Your first stop is the main branch of your public library, where the reference department should carry all the resources mentioned in this chapter. Your second stop is your college's career planning office.

The Standard Industrial Classification (SIC) Manual and/or SIC database are great places to get started. In the SIC directories, corporations are assigned a four-digit code (known as the SIC code) based on the type of industry they are in and the product or service they provide.

Let's say you have a chemical engineering degree and wish to get into the paint and coatings industry. With the SIC code, you can sort through the database of the appropriate industrial directory and locate the names and addresses of all the manufacturing companies that specialize in paints and coatings. Half an hour on the library

computer can produce a list of dozens, if not hundreds, of companies that you can target.

Another way of getting the contact information you need is through a state industrial directory. These are usually updated annually, giving you the most recent phone numbers, addresses, and names and titles of the company principals such as the president, treasurer, vice president of sales, vice president of engineering, and human resources director.

If you have a marketing degree and want a position in account management or sales, address your cover letter and resume to the vice president of sales and marketing. If you're looking for an internal auditing job, contact the vice president of finance, the comptroller, or the treasurer. If no name is given, pick up the phone, call the company, and ask who heads the specific department that interests you.

You might also get contact names and numbers by circulating your targeted company list to friends and family who work in professional capacities. Perhaps they'll recognize the company or know the industry well enough to give you a contact name. You'll have a better chance at the inside track through a personal introduction.

Decentralize, decentralize, decentralize.

Never limit your focus to the company's corporate headquarters. Many manufacturing facilities in the Fortune 500 have more than one location in more than one state, and most service-oriented companies are highly decentralized. That means if a company has 57 branches, all 57 branches have the capability to interview and hire. Send out 57 resumes, one to each targeted manager in each branch. You can see that your odds of securing an interview are automatically increased greatly!

In addition to the SIC Manual and state industrial directories, there are many other business directories available at most libraries. Better yet, in most cases you'll have a choice of sourcing the information in print, via CD-ROM, or online.

To determine which directories are most helpful and easiest to use, ask your local librarian. Basically, all the directories provide contact information, sales volume, number of employees, company principals, etc. They differ based on the size of the companies being profiled or the breakdown of information based on geography or the type of industry.

I recommend any one or more of the following directories to get you rolling:

BUSINESS DIRECTORIES

- Standard & Poor's Register of Corporations, Executives and Industries (Standard & Poor's Corporation—Annual with updates). Also produced in online and CD-ROM formats.

- Million Dollar Directory (Dun's Marketing Services—Annual). Also produced in electronic formats with the online version available exclusively through DIALOG.

- Ward's Business Directory of U.S. Private and Public Companies (Gale Research, Inc.—Annual). Also produced in online and CD-ROM formats.

- Thomas Register of American Manufacturers (Thomas Publishing Company—Annual). Also produced as an online database and a CD-ROM disk.

- Macmillan Directory of Leading Private Companies (National Register Publishing Company—Annual).

- Online Information Network (American Business Information, Inc.—Monthly)

- U.S. Manufacturer's Directory (American Business Information, Inc.—Annual).

- Reference Book of Manufacturers (Dun & Bradstreet Credit Services—Semiannual).

Fear of phoning (and how to overcome it)

The telephone is an extremely valuable networking tool, but you have to know how to use it.

Let me back up. The telephone is an extremely valuable networking tool, but first you have to *use* it!

Many people do well at creating their networking base but then freeze when it comes to using the phone. Personally, I think what stops them is fear of anticipated rejection, not fear of the act of picking up the receiver and dialing the number.

Of course, you will meet rejection in the phone phase of networking. Expect it. When you start calling targeted companies, you'll discover quickly that it's pretty tough to get past some of those receptionists, even when you ask for the department manager by name.

Quite a few companies have firm policies not to release the names and titles of their employees, particularly management, to callers. So if you're phoning to obtain a manager's title and name, you may meet with even more resistance.

Since the company's reason for withholding the information has nothing to do with you personally, don't take the rejection to heart. They're trying to prevent people like me—recruiters—from stealing their key people!

Dealing with gatekeepers

You'll get an idea of how to get past the operator and over your phone fear with some of the following dialogue examples.

"First National Bank. This is Kelly."

"Hello, Kelly. I'm trying to reach the manager of your internal audit department. Can you tell me who that is?"

"What's the nature of the call, please?"

Don't tell Kelly you're looking for a job. She'll immediately transfer you to the human resources department! You can safely assume from the counter question that you're probably not going to get through to the department manager on this call. So you respond in one of two ways.

1. "I'd like to direct some correspondence to the internal audit manager's attention and want to make sure I have the proper title and correct spelling of the name."

2. Or, "Well, Kelly, I'm working on a research project and am hoping to get some information on the banking industry from the perspective of management, specifically the internal audit manager."

Either one of these explanations will usually yield, at the very least, the manager's name and title. With that information in hand, it never hurts to go for broke. Always attempt to get a direct connection.

"Thank you very much for your help. Do you know if Mr. Sellers is available for me to talk with now?"

If the receptionist says "no," simply hang up and call back within the next few days and ask for the manager by name. When you know the receptionist's name, make a note of it and use it on your next call.

Most individuals like to hear their names when people call in. Your odds of getting through to the manager will increase when you call back in a couple of days and say, "Good afternoon, Kelly. Could you please connect me with Roger Sellers?"

Kelly wants to process calls quickly at the switchboard and, hearing her name, she is more likely to assume you are a regular caller and will just put you through to the manager.

Any time the receptionist is willing to put your call through, take the initiative to ask for the person's direct phone line.

"Thanks so much, Kelly. Would it be possible to get Mr. Sellers' direct extension in case I get disconnected and have to call back?"

TRAPS TO AVOID

It takes a lot of work to get a person's direct extension. So don't jot these valuable numbers on flimsy scraps of paper that you're likely to lose (a mistake some of my clients have made). Keep a separate notebook or computer file marked "contacts" and save yourself the trouble of jumping through those phone hoops again.

Dealing with voice mail: "Please make a note of it."

"For technical service, press one. For customer service, press two. To order an elephant and have it delivered overnight, press three...."

Voice mail systems are everywhere, and they have their uses, but luckily there's also a real receptionist lurking behind most of them. If your first call to the company is answered electronically, press "0" for

Operator immediately, and in most cases you'll be connected with a live person. This tactic will reduce your phone time and your bill, not to mention your frustration level.

Some systems also let you press the first few letters of a person's last name to get the full name and extension on a recording—all the more reason to search those business directories for key names. The correct spelling gets you the direct extension, and now you can use the automated system instead of the receptionist each time you call.

A direct call may end up being transferred to a secretary. This is another layer of protection for the busy manager and another opportunity for you to conquer rejection. Be polite yet persistent, and handle yourself as you did with the receptionist. You're getting closer and are likely to get through on the next call, if not on this one.

My inside trick when all else fails

Eventually you'll encounter a receptionist who absolutely, positively refuses to give you the department manager's name or phone number. Don't give up. You can still get the information you need in a roundabout way. Let me share a trick I learned in recruiting that will work just as well for you.

Call the receptionist a day or two later and simply say, "Sales department, please." Asking for the purchasing department or customer service also works. Those are three types of calls receptionists automatically put through without question because they assume you're a customer or a supplier.

Now comes the slightly sneaky part. No matter who answers the phone, you say, "Sales? Oh, I'm sorry, I'm trying to reach Mr. Sellers in your audit department. Can you transfer me, please?"

Unlike the receptionist, employees at large are not trained to ask about the nature of your call. They simply reach for their employee phone directory, look up the extension (don't forget to ask for it before they transfer you!), and put your call through. It works like a charm!

When to call and what to say

The best time to make your calls is between 7:30 a.m. and 9:00 a.m. (These hours may vary in different cities—Chicago is an "early" city, for instance, while New York tends to start later but work longer). The idea is to reach managers early, as they're organizing their desks and their calendar before the day's onslaught. With their name and direct extension, you can call before the company officially opens and catch them before they get involved in their daily routine.

When you make the phone connection, explain that you're trying to secure your first career position in their industry and you'd like to meet with them in a brief, informal interview. Let them know you're interested in their field and you would simply like to ask some questions in order to learn more about the position or industry.

WAKE-UP CALL

My last suggestion regarding the telephone is to use it but not abuse it. If you are overly aggressive, it can work against you just as easily as it can work for you. For busy managers—which is to say every manager—phone calls are distractions and interruptions. Be judicious. And by all means, after making initial phone contact and following up with a resume, *don't* call every other day to see if it has arrived yet.

Even if you don't succeed in getting in the door, you've verbally introduced yourself and have shown an above-average level of motivation. When you follow up the call by sending your resume to the manager's attention, you have a much better chance of being remembered in a favorable light.

There's a fine line between being persistent and becoming a pest. Persistence pays off. It's quite acceptable to follow up with more than one call to the manager to signal your continuing interest. However, you should time the calls appropriately, allowing a few weeks between each one. You'll achieve top-of-mind awareness with the manager without making yourself a nuisance.

These tips should make your telephone networking much easier, but you're still not going to get through to your targeted manager every time with every company. If you're working with a list of 50 companies and one of them won't cooperate, don't take the rejection personally. Continue to call the remaining 49. You might end up being rejected by ten. The trick is to not focus on your rejections but on your 40 successes!

Actually, I think you'll be very surprised at how accommodating people can be. Don't forget, they were once in your shoes. You can often strike a chord by playing on their empathy.

Tapping the resources of family and friends

The people in your personal and social circles can be enormously helpful in your job search. But it shouldn't appear as if they're too helpful. I recommend that you use personal contacts for introductions only. Don't rely on them to get you interviews. If your parents are professionals, for example, by all means use them as networking resources but for introductory purposes only. The connection ends when they hand you a contact name. Work independently to secure the interview.

By doing the legwork yourself, instead of leaving it to Mom or Dad—and by legwork I mean sending your resume and cover letter and following through—you'll be held in much higher regard by the interviewer. If you let Dad drop off your resume and Mom make your calls, you conjure up another kind of impression.

Your well-meaning, well-employed parents may want to set up an interview for you at their company. The idea is to land the interview yourself and treat it like any other. Even if you know the company has a nepotism clause and you have no chance of working there, interview to the best of your ability. This creates secondary networking, which is a very good thing. If your interviewer likes you but can't hire you because your father is employed by the company, you may very well generate another good contact. If you make a good impression, the interviewer won't have any qualms about recommending you to another company.

Don't limit the scope of your networking to your own parents. Use your friends' parents to gain corporate connections. If you know someone whose parent works in an industry that appeals to you, ask that friend to make an introduction. Treat the meeting like an interview, even if takes place in your friend's family room.

By making a good impression, you're improving your chances of getting a foot in the door. Also, you don't have to worry about being discounted for a position because of nepotism. Your chances of landing an interview or an offer are sometimes actually greater when you network through the parent of a friend.

Maximizing the use of your professional associations and affiliations

This is usually a limited networking tool for someone who's only been out of college a year or two. But always make the most of what you've got.

A sidenote on lectures: Seek out programs given by people in the business community, preferably in your desired field. Listen, learn, and introduce yourself to the speaker afterward. Ask a question or two, soft-sell a few of your strengths if appropriate, and offer a copy of your resume. Get the person's business card and follow up in a week or so with a phone call or letter. It's a polite, often effective way to network.

You should also conduct a little research to learn about all the professional organizations in your chosen career path. There are thousands, and often several within a single industry: the American Pro-

DAMAGE CONTROL

Maybe you took the trouble to join a professional association in college. Smart move. But maybe you lacked the time or inclination to start networking before you graduated. Not so smart. Still, it's not too late to leverage your membership. As an alumnus, you can participate by getting active now. Attend lectures, help with mailings, offer to lend a hand in whatever way is needed.

duction and Inventory Control Society (APICS), Society of Mechanical Engineers, American Marketing Association, Chemical Manufacturer's Association, American Society of Quality Control, American Society of Materials, Society of Women Engineers, Society of Black Engineers, and National Association of Purchasing Management are just a few examples. They're listed by subject in the annual *Directory of Associations,* published by Gale Research and available in major libraries.

Pinpoint a few organizations of interest, then call or write them for more information. Find out what it takes to become a member or to achieve certification, and follow through if the requirements are within the realm of possibility. Also, ask the organization's staff and members for the names and contact information of other professionally related groups—that's one form of a smart tactic I call "second-sourcing."

In the same vein, subscribe to newsletters or publications in your field, or seek out specialized libraries that carry them. Be sure you're on the subscription list for your professional organization (sometimes there's an additional charge). Many professionally employed members use these media to post job openings. You'll also glean information about your future field, along with names and titles of key people and information about the companies they work for.

You have nothing to lose and everything to gain by becoming active in a professional society early in your job search. Gathering more knowledge of the industry will improve your interviewing skills, and the professional connections you make might very well result in landing you an interview. Plus, the initiative you show by getting active early makes quite a positive impression on a prospective employer.

Surfing the Internet

Cyberspace is a fast-expanding horizon for recruitment and job search. Steps have already been made to electronically market candidates to employers and vice versa.

As an example, I work with the Association of Graduates (AOG) through West Point Military Academy. The AOG distributes diskettes containing the resumes of hundreds of past graduates who are either entering the job market or want to make a career change. I can also post current job openings online with the AOG, accessible to all graduates who choose to search the job database.

As cyber consciousness grows, colleges and universities are gearing up with capabilities like these. I strongly suggest you check with your college placement office to see if this type of service is available to you.

Another suggestion is to see if your university provides alumni access to the Internet and/or online services such as Prodigy, America Online, and CompuServe. Many do, often at no cost, although the university may limit your online time so as to provide maximum access to all users.

Through my own experience on the Internet I've discovered quite an array of online career networking services such as CareerNet, CareerWEB, and CareerMosaic, to name just a few. In addition, most major corporations now have web pages where you can find their current job openings as well as up-to-date information about the company and products. Most also offer the opportunity to submit your resume via e-mail or fax.

The best and quickest way to access this information is through the use of a web navigator, e.g., Netscape, or "search engines" such as Web Crawler, Yahoo, etc. Simply enter keywords for the companies, industries, or job titles you'd like to access and let the navigator do the work for you.

Surf the Internet and World Wide Web and you're sure to discover all kinds of career services. New ones are coming online every day. Check them out. I also suggest you upload your resume onto the system whenever the opportunity presents itself. You're circulating your credentials worldwide for free or for pennies. It can't hurt.

Doing online research

Some online providers give you access to newspaper want ads in other cities, ideal for relocators. (That's you, right?) If you're living in Pittsburgh and yearn for the bright lights of Los Angeles or New York, it's an excellent way to check out the job market without leaving your home or campus.

Cyberspace is a gold mine for all types of research. I'm sure you noticed that most of the business directories recommended earlier in this chapter are available online. In addition, you can use the Internet or online services to locate current magazine and newspaper articles relating to a specific company or industry that interests you. Such literature searches, as they're called, are not always free—the cost of browsing through and/or printing out articles can add up. But there's no better way to get up to speed quickly when preparing for an interview. You may uncover late-breaking information that you'd never find elsewhere.

At this point, I can't predict how the Internet will affect recruitment in the twenty-first century. Will we be exchanging resumes by e-mail and interviewing through video hookups? Cyberspace and face-to-face contact each has its unique strengths, so I don't think the old-fashioned methods will disappear. But I do believe that the Internet is a tremendous resource and an opportunity to access a wealth of information.

7

The Resume

Will Yours Open Doors or Line Trash Cans?

What do resumes have to do with doughnuts?

Thousands and thousands of resumes have crossed my desk. Some I'll never forget, not because they were good but because they were bad, and in many cases, just plain weird.

One in particular that comes to mind was a three-page letter written in a warm, friendly, and familiar style with a lot of "down home" flavor. I read it in its entirety because it was … what's a good word? Let's call it *different*.

The young man told me about working on a farm while going to college, expressed his love for farms and the serenity of a rural setting, shared with me his fondness for animals, and invited me to meet him at his place for an informal interview over coffee and doughnuts.

He thought we could get to know each other better in a more personal setting.

Although I don't imagine it was the writer's intent, this "resume" generated a lot of laughs. But it didn't result in a job, an interview, or even a shared plate of doughnuts.

The objective of an effective resume is not to be weird or different. Weird and off-the-wall will land you in the paper shredder or the round file, but it won't land you an interview. What you say about yourself on that piece of paper and how you present it have to be good enough to get you in the door.

So, what makes a resume work for you instead of against you? For starters, let's talk about what *doesn't* work.

That elusive document: An error-free resume

As I said before, recruiters like me receive literally thousands of resumes. And we find thousands of mistakes on them that shouldn't have been made by a kid in junior high, much less a college graduate.

Resume mistakes: An honor roll

1. Quite a few resumes arrive with no phone numbers or incorrect phone numbers. Hello?

2. The sad truth: Many resumes are riddled with misspelled words and poor grammar, even from English majors.

3. I see resumes that look as if they had been used to clean a windshield before being mailed. I get them on fluorescent-colored paper, peppered with clever computer graphics, sometimes printed in three or four different typefaces or fonts.

TRAPS TO AVOID

Unless you're applying to work at *Wired* magazine, tone down your efforts at visual hypercreativity. Words that dance around against a neon-green background are an assault, not an attention-getter.

4. Last-minute thoughts pop up on a lot of resumes. If your handwritten P.S. or inked-in correction was important enough to mention at all, isn't it important enough to be printed rather than scrawled on?

5. This one may be my absolute favorite. Some resumes arrive with postage due! By all means, remember the stamp.

The bottom line is that, sometimes, what makes a resume good enough to get you in the door is simply the fact that it's error-free. And the mistakes I've just outlined aren't even the most common and avoidable ones. Later in this chapter you'll discover the *major* resume mistakes!

The look of your resume speaks volumes.

Please, treat your resume as a professional calling card. It's an extension of you and a reflection of your basic skills. If it's sloppily put together, it sends a message that you're not very conscientious about your work. If it lacks phone numbers, significant dates, or that all-important postage stamp, it says that you don't have much of an eye for detail.

Misspellings and poor grammar signal weak written communication skills. And when you fail to record the dates of employment and education properly (or at all), the reader will think you're trying to hide something.

So you see, your resume says a lot about you ... both good and bad. And the more good things you have to say about yourself, both in terms of the visual and the credentials, the more likely it is that you'll land the interview. Here are a few pointers to help you design a resume that works for you, makes you more marketable, and opens up those interviewing doors.

There are differing opinions among personnel consultants and recruiters about the importance of stating a career objective on your resume. Some say you don't need one; most say you do. I run with the majority and think the objective is a key part of the resume.

How you present your objective is also very important. Recruiters don't all agree on that subject either. My advice here is geared to a first-time job seeker. The rules are just a little different than they are for someone with fifteen years of experience.

Some recruiters say that if you want to be an auditor, your objective should say so. Of course, the same holds true if you want to be a retail manager or a design engineer. I think that's smart advice for someone who is already an auditor and wants to switch companies, or for a person in the retail industry ready to move into management, or for an engineer looking for a new product to design. You get the idea.

For a recent grad, however, being too specific in your career objective can work against you.

The joys of ambiguity

I recommend being "specifically vague" when presenting your career objective.

College grads come to me searching for a career. Some have no experience so they're hoping to find a training program. Most want to work for a large, reputable company, or better yet, a Fortune 500 with opportunities for advancement. And for many, that's about all they know—even at this stage of the game.

WAKE-UP CALL

Like most people, you want "a good job." But do you know what you can or should be doing? What kind of company or industry you belong in? Where to locate what you want?

You're reading this book to find some answers, and that's wonderful. In the meantime, however, it's hard to be specific about your career objective if you lack the necessary information. That's why "specifically vague" works like a charm.

"My objective is to secure an entry-level position with a major corporation offering opportunities for growth and advancement." How's that for specifically vague? You're not pigeonholing yourself, yet you're being very precise in communicating what you want.

Your resume should indicate the school you attended, the month and year of graduation, your major (and minor, if applicable) and grade point average. Do not list the names and code numbers of the classes you've taken. That information is irrelevant and just takes up valuable space.

Listing your GPA can be tricky. If you don't indicate your grade point average on the resume, the employer will *assume* it's low or below 3.0. If your overall GPA is lower than a 3.0 and your GPA in your major is a little higher, then put your major GPA on the resume and omit the overall.

Example:
Purdue University, Purdue, Indiana 5/97
Bachelor of Science in Business Administration
Major: Finance (3.2)
Minor: Accounting (3.0)

In this example, the overall GPA might be 2.8 or lower. If the company has a 3.0 cutoff, as so many do, you will have avoided elimination by presenting it this way. Get the interview first and then you'll be able to explain to the employer why your overall GPA was a little lower. Perhaps you worked 30 hours a week or you were actively involved in lots of extracurricular activities. At any rate, you'll have the chance to overcome the objection.

Sorry, but 2.7 does not equal 3.0.

One more vital warning about your grade point average. It's okay to round 2.67 up to 2.7, but you're not going to get away with rounding it up to 3.0. Yes, $2.67 can and should be reported as $3.00 when you're claiming an expense on your income tax form—but recruiters see things differently from the IRS.

Remember, most corporations will eventually ask you to produce a copy of your college transcripts. Some employers will even verify high school transcripts. So, if your memory is faulty, say so. Don't "guesstimate."

TRAPS TO AVOID

Some people like to highlight their high school education on the resume. In my opinion, you're better off using the precious space to emphasize work history, college activities, or special skills. The only exceptions are high school items that might set you apart from the crowd. Were you valedictorian or salutatorian? Did you study abroad? Did you attend a prestigious prep school? Anything else is just "filler."

About internships and externships

The education section of your resume is also the place to include foreign study, exchange programs with other universities, or any externships. Those are corporate-sponsored programs conducted at the college or university and usually done in the style of a group case study. They're not the same as internships, nor do they have equal importance to an employer. An externship is more along the lines of a college class with the corporation providing the educators and classroom agenda.

I've seen a lot of resumes with internships highlighted along with college credentials. Personally, I think an internship has more impact when it's included in the work history section of the resume. More on that later.

Dollars and sense

Did you pay 50 percent or more of the cost of your education? If so, trumpet that fact on your resume. Employers look favorably on candidates who have earned their learning. The more you contributed, the better you appear in terms of motivation, work ethic, and sense of responsibility.

When computing the percentage you contributed, be fair to yourself. The cost of an education is more than tuition and books. Calculate living expenses, travel, food, entertainment, and the like. Also, don't discount your scholarships (you earned them!) or any grants or loans you have to repay, including parental loans.

Honors and activities: Gold stars

This portion of the resume emphasizes your awards for academic excellence (Honoraries, Dean's List, President's List, etc.), scholarships, clubs, organizations, fraternity and sorority affiliations, and any offices held.

Honors and activities should include any community service or participation in charitable organizations. It is also the area where you'll highlight your involvement in organized athletics, whether through the university or those sponsored by the city in which you live. If you were a captain or co-captain, say so. If you lettered, mention that too.

Work history: Odd jobs are okay.

Do you match the following work profile?

A variety of odd jobs through summer and winter breaks; working one month here, three months there, in restaurants, lawn service companies, amusement parks, telemarketing jobs; no work experience in any field related to the career you might be pursuing, unless you've been fortunate enough to have an internship.

Sure, those jobs meant money, but will they help you for the future?

You'll be relieved to know that recruiters regard work history and
work experience as two entirely different things. At the entry level,
most corporations recruit trainees based on the candidate's potential,
not necessarily on their related experience. They determine your potential by how hard you worked at what you did, how quickly you
learned the job, what basic skills you learned in the job, and if you
were given additional responsibilities and promotions.

Most recent grads have a tendency to "play" with the work history
on their resumes. In my experience working with recruits, I've wit-
nessed some pretty creative methods of embellishing the resume. I
want to share with you what I've learned so you can avoid making the
same mistakes.

The four most common and avoidable resume mistakes

Also known as "The Major Mistakes," these *cost* you.

Major resume mistake #1: Omitting jobs you feel are insignificant

You spent a summer flipping hamburgers at McDonald's, edging
lawns, or busing tables. Granted, these are not the most glamorous
jobs. But by not mentioning them on your resume, regardless of the positions held, you create a gap in your employment record. And "gap" is
not a good word in this context. The employer would rather see that
you worked at *something,* as opposed to the alternative, which is that
you didn't work at all. Besides, everything you've done to this point has
resulted in your being who you are today.

If you bagged fries at a fast-food chain, you've developed some
very important people skills and have probably enhanced your verbal
communication skills. If your landscaping stint put you in charge of six
high school kids, you've shown potential for leadership and management. If you waited on or bused tables, you learned how to work well
under pressure.

In other words, your *job description* and how you developed are
more significant to potential employers than who you worked for or
how long you were employed there. That's why the work history section of your resume should include a brief description of your responsibilities and the skills you developed in each position. Simply listing
the employer's name and dates of employment is a mistake. It wastes
an opportunity to sell yourself.

Major resume mistake #2: Padding employment

Major mistake #1 almost always leads to major mistake #2. The fatal thought process goes this way: *Decide not to list no-brainer job. Realize I have gap in employment. Want to fill gap. So exaggerate the time spent on my other, better jobs.*

Entirely understandable. But a big, big, big trap!

Employers *do* check references. You might think that your "reference" will cover your work habits, punctuality, personality, and the like. It rarely will. These days, the name of the reference game is employment dates.

There have been so many lawsuits over references that most companies now provide only your starting and ending dates of employment. That's all. These dates verify your employment. Being unadorned by any other information, they stand out in stark relief.

So if you "pad" your employment dates, you're setting your own trap. Potential employers have a name for padding: they call it *lying*. And lies alone are enough to ruin your chances for another interview, or worse yet, an offer.

Major resume mistake #3: The "keep 'em guessing" approach

Quite a few people think it's to their advantage to leave off the months and indicate only the years of employment on their resume. For example:

1995 to 1996   Mellon Bank, Pittsburgh, PA
Bank Teller
Responsibilities included customer service and
problem solving. Developed an eye for detail and
the ability to work well independently.

If given a chance to draw a conclusion about you from this information, employers will almost always draw a negative conclusion. Remember, they are conditioned to "screen out" candidates. If they have 500 resumes and want to interview ten people, *they look for reasons to eliminate 490!* Don't give them a reason.

Most recruiters, myself included, would conclude you worked at Mellon Bank from December 1995 to January 1996. That's two months, or maybe even two weeks! Of course, you might have started in January 1995 and worked until December 1996, which is two *years*. But if you did have two years of experience in this job, surely you'd indicate as much.

Dishonesty lurks behind fuzziness. Rightly or wrongly, recruiters and employers assume that inexact dates are meant to hide something. Keeping the employer guessing will do nothing but keep you out of interviews.

Major resume mistake #4: Exercising creativity with your job description and title

I once got a resume from a young woman who worked at a major department store during her Christmas break. Her major was Adver-

LOOKING AHEAD

You don't need me to tell you there is no Santa Claus. But part of my job is to bust some grown-up myths.

Any misleading information about your background will eventually come back to haunt you. Don't embellish and don't lie, unless you want to sabotage yourself. This is proven advice for any stage of your career. (Keep it in mind when you're a CEO.)

Scrutinize your resume. If you've padded or gotten too creative, open that file. Your delete key is about to enjoy a heavy workout.

Yes, sometimes "honest" can seem boring. But when your resume is accurate and thorough, you can't go wrong.

tising and Public Relations, and she listed her job title as Public Relations Assistant.

With the same fervor she might have used to describe the designing of an ad campaign for Nike, this person wrote a long paragraph outlining her duties as ... a Christmas Elf.

An elf is an elf, not a Public Relations Assistant. I understand that Ms. Elf was trying to link her experience to her major studies and targeted career path, but there are limits. Remember, you're writing a resume, not a fairy tale.

Internships and how to maximize them. One easy way to turbocharge your resume, in my opinion, is to include any internships under "work history" rather than "education." For most grads, the internship is the only relative work history they have, so it should be given the attention it deserves.

With major resume mistake #4 fresh in our minds, let me emphasize that any listed internships should be real ones. Maybe you spent a summer working for a corporation as a temp or clerical employee. That's fine, but it doesn't count as a bona fide internship. And if you try to pass it off as such, a few well-targeted questions in the interview will blow your cover.

Internships are significant because the tasks assigned the intern usually have a greater degree of responsibility than those assigned to temp-type employees. Make sure you note the skills you've developed as a result of completing your assignment.

Another distinguishing feature is that internships are not easy to come by. In Chapter 2, I recommended that underclassmen and those pursuing an advanced degree try to secure an internship at any cost, even if it means working for free. If you're one of those go-getters, by all means indicate on your resume that it was an unpaid position.

You've heard this before, but employers can't hear it often enough: Your internship (especially if unpaid) indicates that you have an excellent work ethic, high level of motivation, goal orientation, and a willingness to pay prices to get what you want out of life.

All of these qualities set you apart from your competition.

Military service: Saluting Uncle Sam. Military service carries a lot of weight with certain employers. Take advantage of that by highlighting your achievements. You've earned them.

If you have served in the military in any capacity, present the information on your resume after the work history. If you have no work history outside the military, or your other jobs are less significant, then your military experience should be listed instead of, or ahead of, your work experience.

Indicate your length of service, always citing month and year, and include position titles and job descriptions. If you received any honors, awards, or promotions—or if you served outside the United States—this information should follow your positions and job descriptions. Don't include these accomplishments in the honors and activities section preceding the work history. You want to keep your academic honors separate from those earned in the military.

Additional information: All that "other stuff"

Not everything about a job candidate fits neatly into the categories outlined so far. Other factors may set you apart from the crowd or help the employer recognize your suitability to their company or position. I'll suggest a few possibilities, but only you can evaluate their importance in your own situation.

WAKE-UP CALL

Why is your resume like the island of Manhattan? Because it's a piece of real estate where every spare inch is worth a fortune. When composing or revising yours, constantly ask yourself: Is this piece of information truly worth the space it will occupy?

Fun with hobbies

It's fine to include a line on your resume for hobbies and special interests, if that pleases you. This sort of thing can be an icebreaker. The world seems a little cozier when we cross paths with fellow guitar players, scuba divers, or gourmet cooks.

At the same time, this is the area in which to apply your most stringent "real estate" test. Don't let hobbies rob precious space from another area that requires more attention.

Speaking the language of special skills

It makes sense to list any aptitudes relevant to the positions you're seeking. If you have a Computer Science degree, list the programs in which you are proficient. If you are multilingual, indicate the languages you speak fluently.

Again, I caution you to be honest in your assessment of your special skills. Don't say you're proficient in QuarkXpress if you've had only limited exposure. Don't claim to speak Spanish if the extent of your vocabulary is *adios* and *una cerveza, por favor!*

In recent years, bilingual candidates have been in demand in a lot of major market cities. More and more graduates are becoming aware of this trend and indicating on their resumes that they are fluent in another language. Taking four years of Spanish in high school, or eight years of French in high school and college, does not necessarily make you fluent. Fluency means being able to speak a language and understand it; literacy means being able to read and write it. Foreign language education in this country is notorious for producing students who couldn't really *function* in another language if their jobs depended on it.

TRAPS TO AVOID

When I'm interviewing candidates who say they're bilingual, at some point I casually ask them to answer my next question in their second language.

No one even fakes it. Most of the time I get an excuse—in English—as to why they are rusty. Or a confession that they can understand the language but not speak it.

This trap is so easy to set and it always works. It's just one more reason to be honest about the abilities you claim for yourself.

Availability: When can you start?

If you can spare the space, it's a good idea to let employers know *where* and *when* you can come aboard. Some useful phrases: *open to relocation, can start immediately, available with two-week notice,* or *prefer Mid-Atlantic region.*

References: The good, the bad, and the useless

In my opinion, references are not necessary on a resume for an entry-level candidate. For people with job experience, the right references can help secure an interview. By "right" I mean that the people recommending you, and the companies they work for, should be reputable and have high visibility. But when you're just starting out, references tend to be weak and they take up too much valuable space. Specifically, most recent college grads use professors and previous managers from odd jobs as references. It's unlikely that these will make an impact on the person reading your resume. Other factors will determine whether you secure the interview.

However, I'm not saying you should forget all about references. Quite the contrary. Be prepared to provide them *during* an interview. If the employer asks, you should be equipped with a separate sheet of paper listing three references—each complete with name, professional capacities, address, and phone number.

For each reference, try to include both home and office phone numbers. References are usually checked during business hours, so provide numbers where your references can be reached during those hours.

You need to alert these three people that they might be receiving a call about you. (It's a good opportunity to keep in touch and maybe discover a few job leads as well.) And always, always obtain permission before you list them as references in the first place.

As I mentioned earlier, checking references these days is often just a synonym for verifying employment dates—often, but not always. So it's also wise to ask your references what they're prepared to say about you when contacted—this helps both of you think a little bit more about the matter.

I hope you've scrawled all over this chapter (unless this is a library book), making notes about the fundamentals of your resume. We've covered the Big Three: content, the employer's perception of your presentation, and the pitfalls to avoid. Next let's work on putting it all together to make your resume really work for you.

8

The Resume

Writing One That Works

Resume writing is looked on by most of my clients as a necessary evil. In fact, thinking it was part of my service, most of them expected *me* to write their resumes for them. Surprise! What they got was a lesson on how to do it themselves. In my opinion, you are the person who will do the best job at this essential task. At most you'll need a little guidance and practical advice.

I've had clients who have shelled out $100 or more to professional resume-writing services. Almost without exception, these high-ticket documents have been some of the worst looking and most poorly written examples that have ever crossed my desk. Believe me, no one knows you or can sell you better than yourself. Don't pay someone to write your resume; put that money toward an interviewing suit instead. Read this chapter and take a crack at writing your own resume. It's just not that difficult.

I've fictionalized the names on these illustrative resumes, but all job descriptions, college credentials, and personal histories are word-for-word fact. I haven't mixed-and-matched information to make anyone's life easier. These are real resumes with the names changed strictly to protect privacy.

The significant point is that all five resumes worked well enough to land interviews and, ultimately, job offers for my former clients.

GOOD NEWS

You may be reassured to hear a recruiter say that one size does *not* fit all resumes. The form is flexible, within limits. In fact, since each person has a unique educational background and work history, a single model would never work. So, in this chapter I'll show you a variety of effective resumes, each one very different, and all from former clients.

I purposely chose the resumes of five candidates who did not build a perfect set of credentials during college. As first-time job seekers, most of these people lacked at least one essential ingredient for smooth sailing. But all of them learned how to use the resume to overcome what they lacked.

As you pore over the resumes, note that the candidates' backgrounds are a very mixed bag. Each demanded its own unique presentation.

The idea is not to copy these resumes, but to review them, reading my follow-up comments, to get an idea of how to create a resume that works for you. (If the resume gets you interviews, it works!)

Order on the page

First, some general guidelines. There's a basic order to follow when designing your resume—name, address, and contact information, objective, education, honors and activities, work history, military background, and miscellaneous—but you'll need to apply common sense. You may need to alter the sequence of information to highlight your particular strengths.

Brevity is very important. Think *short*. Always, always, *always* keep the resume to one page. If necessary, play with your margins or use a smaller typeface (but not too small to read easily). Most recent college graduates should be able to accomplish this pretty easily since they don't have much experience to document. In fact, one of the reasons professionally prepared resumes are so bad is because they are usually so long.

TRAPS TO AVOID

A book-style, four-page resume is a popular format I've been seeing lately. In my firm opinion, anything beyond one page is overkill for a recent college graduate.

If your credentials are so extensive that you feel you need a second page, then keep your resume to a single sheet by printing on both sides. When your resume is too long, you should ask yourself what's eating up the space. I'd estimate that in five years I've met only a handful of recent graduates who truly *needed* two pages for their resumes.

There's another way to let the employer know whatever it is about your background that you couldn't fit on the resume. It's the cover letter, and no resume is complete without one! (More on this in Chapter 9.)

Charlie Collidge did all the right things in getting his education. He got good grades, worked during the school year, had an internship related to his degree, was active in extracurriculars, was willing to relocate, and indicated he had continuous employment since graduating from high school. He did a great job of creating an excellent entry-level resume. As a recruiter, I'd regard Charlie as a highly desirable candidate.

Let's dissect Charlie's credentials and how he presents them. First, look at his work history. The rule here is to list your current or most recent employer first, then proceed backward in time. This rule doesn't always apply for someone just out of college.

Because most graduates have very little corporate work history, what they *do* have should be given the attention it deserves. If you have one or two internships and all your other work history is noncorporate (e.g., in restaurants or department stores), list your internships *first* and follow them with your most recent or current employment as this young man did.

Second, while Charlie is an accounting major, he is not necessarily interested only in accounting. He *may* want to pursue certification in accounting—but saying so on the resume may screen him out of certain positions. Whether to include such information depends entirely upon what you're looking for.

In this resume, Charlie's objective and internship make it clear he's interested in more than pure accounting. When he first came to me, however, his original resume stated his objective as "finding an accounting-related" position. He even indicated he was studying for his CPA. With those words on paper, Charlie would have put himself out of the running for corporate audit or analysis positions. He probably would never have gotten an interview no matter how good his credentials were. Here's why. Since most people pursuing CPA status want to work in public accounting or start their own business, major corporations are hesitant to hire them as internal audit trainees. The risk is too high that the person will leave and the investment will be lost.

That doesn't mean you can't mention such possibilities or aspirations. The place to do it, though, is in an *interview*. There you're able to explain your motivation for wanting to be certified, or whatever. But when an employer merely reads it on a resume, you're not there to "defend" yourself against an employer's assumptions.

As always, don't give recruiters any reasons not to call *you*!

William Payer: Compensating for weaknesses

Bill Payer got his master's degree the right way but the hard way. He graduated, landed a corporate accounting position in a bank, got over a year of experience, and then returned to school. He not only postponed a great career but had to work as a waiter to pay for his advanced degree.

Charles E. Collidge
1338 Mulberry Lane
Albuquerque, New Mexico 87101
505-555-1919

Objective: To obtain a position in the field of accounting, finance, or audit with a progressive company offering opportunities for growth and advancement.

Education: The University of New Mexico, Albuquerque 5/93
Bachelor of Science in Business Administration
Graduated Summa Cum Laude (3.91/4.0)
Major: Finance
Minor: Accounting
Responsible for 75% of educational expenses

Honors & Activities: Member, Phi Gamma Delta fraternity. Served as Rush Chairman ('90), Social Chairman ('91), President ('92). Member, National Accounting Association ('91 & '92), Young Business Leader's Organization ('92). Recipient of Red & Gray Scholarship, Kiwanis Scholarship and YMCA Scholarship.

Work History: Best Bank, Albuquerque, NM 1/93–4/93
Internship, Internal Audit
Responsibilities included posting accounts using Lotus 1-2-3, audit of financial statements and interfacing with many of the bank's departments and branches. Required analytical problem solving, strong interpersonals and an eye for detail.

Frank's Hardware Store 5/89–present
Assistant Manager
Began as a clerk and was promoted after one year. Developed excellent customer service and communication skills. Responsible for managing and motivating a staff of eight. Since 6/93, I've been responsible for overseeing all accounting up to and including the general ledger. Employed full-time summers, part-time during school.

Special Skills: Proficient in Lotus 1-2-3, WordPerfect, and QuattroPro with a working knowledge of C and Pascal.

Availability: Willing to relocate. Available with two-week notice.
References provided upon request.

William Payer
1515 Ningia Blvd.
Snohomish, WA 98290
(206) 555-8989

OBJECTIVE: To obtain a challenging position in corporate finance utilizing my education and experience in accounting and offering opportunities for growth into management.

EDUCATION: Master of Business Administration, Finance
University of Washington, Seattle, 8/93 to 12/94

BSBA, Accounting (3.5 GPA), 12/91
Edinboro University, Edinboro, Pennsylvania

EXPERIENCE:
3/92 - 7/93

Albaraka Bancorp, Inc., Pasadena, California
Staff Accountant

- Monitored and kept records in general ledger, accounts receivable and payable, and payroll accounting.
- Prepared monthly financial statements and analyzed prospective investments.
- Performed extensive work in Lotus 1-2-3, Enable, WordPerfect 6.0, Microsoft, and numerous other accounting/finance software packages.
- Have learned to work effectively in a team environment, yet work very well independently.
- Developed necessary problem-solving skills and the ability to work well under pressure and improved my organizational skills.

7/93-PRESENT
AND
5/89-2/92

T.G.I. Friday, various locations
Have been employed 25-30 hours a week in a variety of restaurant-related positions including busboy, waiter, and bartender in order to contribute to the payment of my education. As a result, I've developed great time management skills, excellent communication skills, and am able to get along well with all types of people.

SPECIAL
ACHIEVEMENTS:

Edinboro Academic Scholarship, 4 years Dean's list
Eagle Scout
Paid 100% of all college-related expenses

ADDITIONAL
INFORMATION:

Willing to travel and/or relocate. Available immediately.
References furnished on request.

Bill has no extracurriculars because he spent so much time working to pay the bills and studying to keep his grades up. His GPA in his master's program is 3.0, which isn't great. In fact, it's the minimum required to earn the degree. That's why Bill chose to omit his master's GPA and include only his bachelor's GPA, which was much higher. Most employers would correctly assume that Bill has strong academic ability but has just spread himself a little too thin.

Without extracurriculars, Bill has no Honors and Activities section. He compensates by focusing more attention on his accounting-related experience and work history, and by adding a Special Achievements section to the resume.

Bill Payer crafted his resume to send a strong message about his work ethic, his principles, and his ability to set and achieve goals. The Education section tells me he completed his master's degree six months ahead of schedule. Farther down the page I see that he worked 25 hours a week, which makes his early graduation even more impressive.

Constance Pewter: Overcoming preconceived notions

Connie Pewter has excellent academic credentials but also quite a few negatives in her background. Her resume is designed to overcome those drawbacks.

Connie lacks extracurricular activities, but often mentions that she's a team player who gets along well with others. Those two skills are usually gained through participation in extracurriculars; here Connie shows the employer she's learned them through her various jobs.

Internships are important in the field of programming. Unfortunately, Connie has none. To compensate, she has two years of exposure to computers through her position as lab monitor at the college. The job required her to do a lot of tutoring. Smart recruiters realize that two years of tutoring in many different programs is easily as good experience as a three-month internship working with one or two programs.

Most recruiters assume that someone with a master's degree expects more money and more responsibility. Connie's stated objective does a great job of indicating that her expectations are more reasonable and realistic. Despite holding an advanced degree in Management Information Systems, she's willing to start as an entry-level programmer. That willingness signals an excellent attitude and a high degree of motivation.

WAKE-UP CALL

Many recruiters have preconceived notions about programmers. They're presumed to be below-average communicators and introverts. Connie did a great job of indicating that she has developed good communication and people skills in her jobs, no matter how menial they may have been.

Constance Pewter
788 Penny Lane
Shoreside, New Jersey 08999
908-555-1234

OBJECTIVE
Seeking an entry-level programming position offering opportunities for growth and advancement.

EDUCATION
Master of Science, MIS concentration, 3.64 GPA
Monmouth College, Long Branch, NJ 5/94

EXPERIENCE
Monmouth College, Long Branch, NJ 9/92 to 5/94
Computer Lab Monitor
Responsible for opening and closing of computer lab, providing one-on-one tutoring to students, and monitoring and maintenance of all computer-related equipment. Developed excellent problem-solving skills, people skills and improved communication skills.

Monmouth College, Long Branch, NJ 9/88 to 5/92
Cafeteria Cashier
Position required excellent communication and customer service skills. Responsibilities included the accurate balancing of the cash drawer and daily receipts. Developed excellent time management skills working 25 hours per week and taking full course load.

Shoreside County Recycling Program, Summers, 1988 to 1992
Litter Crew Supervisor
Began as a member of a road clean-up crew and was promoted to supervisor after first summer. Became excellent team player and developed good management skills.

SPECIAL SKILLS
Proficient in C++, C, ADA, Pascal, 88/86 Assembly, ASC and BASIC computer languages. Have programming experience in DOS, UNIX, and VAX operating systems. Also proficient in a wide variety of software packages including Lotus, Symphony, QuattroPro, WordPerfect, Microsoft Word, SPSS, MAS and many others.

HONORS AND AWARDS
Dean's List, All semesters
Valedictorian, Roosevelt High School

ADDITIONAL INFORMATION
100% Relocatable. Paid 50% of college-related expenses. Available to start immediately.

Connie's background implies that she might not want to relocate: She attended a small, local college for six years and all of her jobs were either local or school-affiliated. To counter this impression, her resume clearly indicates her actual willingness to relocate.

The last possible objection to Connie has to do with her work ethic. Most recruiters assume that lab monitoring is a work/study job, which would have required her to work less than 10 hours a week. By adding this assessment to Connie's above-average grades, recruiters might surmise that she spent most of her time studying and very little time on the job. She overcomes that nicely by noting how many hours she worked and the fact that she paid for half of her education.

Connie's resume also raises a good tip to keep in mind. Under Special Skills, she listed some of the programs and software packages in which she is proficient. But she wisely alluded to "many others"—the magic phrase!

When I represent a corporation recruiting an entry-level programmer, I'll scan resumes for references to the exact systems and software used by the employer. When a candidate indicates a partial listing, I'll telephone them for the full listing. Anything on your resume that prompts an employer to want to know more is to your benefit! And every follow-up call may lead to an interview.

Grady Lowe: Accentuating the positive

Grady Lowe has a superior work ethic; not just good, but outstanding, awesome, out of the ordinary. His willingness to pay prices to meet his goals is also evident. Unfortunately, his biggest sacrifice seems to have been his GPA. Recruiters generally assume your GPA is low if it's missing from your resume. The absence of academic honors is another clue; Grady lacks those, too.

Since employers screen out, most would stop reading Grady's resume at that point. Thus it was a smart move for him to indicate under "Education" that he worked full-time. His work ethic is a valid selling point that cancels out the perceived negative surrounding his academic credentials.

Employers are likely to forgive Grady's missing GPA and read on. If he indicated that he worked full time under the "Work History" section, the recruiter might never have read that far down on the page. (Recruiters are busy people who are literally deluged with resumes.)

To further compensate for his grades, Grady used his resume to sell his management potential and leadership skills. He tells employers that he not only worked full-time but also sought out an internship and worked six months for no pay. That's twice the length of an average internship; moreover, he *volunteered* his time. Grady is looking better all the time.

Plus—and this is really rare—he worked for the same employer for seven years! So what if it was McDonald's? Such tenure is so atypical that it really sets Grady apart from the pack. That long stint also speaks well about his character. Grady is likely to be dedicated, loyal, responsible, and probably more mature than his peers.

Grady Lowe
789 Sunnyside Avenue
Toledo, Ohio 43601
419-555-4321

Career Objective

Seeking an entry-level management training program offering advancement potential based on individual merit.

Education

The University of Toledo, Toledo, Ohio
Bachelor of Business Administration, June 1994
Major: Marketing, Minor: Management
Worked 40 hours per week in order to pay 100% of college expenses

Activities

Activities Coordinator, American Red Cross
Organized student volunteers at three universities over spring break to assist in the cleanup following Hurricane Andrew.
Residence Representative, Roosevelt Hall Government
Achieved 100% student participation in all community-service-oriented volunteer activities.
Financial Management Association
Active member 3 out of 4 years. Elected treasurer, 1993/94.
American Marketing Association
Active member 2 years. Elected vice president, 1993/94.

Experience

Fahlgren Martin, Toledo, Ohio, January 1994-June 1994
Internship

- Volunteer intern for 6 months while working full time and attending classes.

- Participated in the preparation of presentations for new and existing clients.

- Spent at least 2 weeks in each department in order to gain an overview of the general management of an advertising agency.

McDonald's, Toledo, Ohio, January 1988-Present
Shift Manager

- Responsible for all activities related to food preparation and customer service.

- Responsible for the training, scheduling, and supervision of up to 25 employees.

- Assisted management in the interviewing, hiring, and training of new employees.

- Have developed excellent management and problem-solving skills.

- Was promoted to shift manager after only five months on the job.

Grady contributed his time to the community and to his extracurricular activities and was elected to positions of leadership or management in both instances. As a recruiter, I'm impressed. Sure, I assume his grades were low, but his other qualities are so good that I'll probably want to interview him.

I applaud Grady for using most of the resume to sell his work ethic and management potential. But to stay within one page—still a cardinal rule—he sacrificed other important points such as availability, willingness to relocate, special skills, and aptitudes.

There are times when omitting information from your resume can keep you from getting an interview. Reading Grady's resume cold, I would assume he is *not* relocatable. He lives in Toledo, went to school there, works there, got his internship there, and says nothing on his resume about being willing to make a change. For a lot of employers, that would be reason enough not to invite Grady to interview. But all is not lost.

Whenever you can't fit vital information on the resume, highlight it in your cover letter. That's exactly what Grady did. His cover letter clearly stated his willingness to move for his career and included other information that might further sell an employer on giving him consideration for an interview.

Joseph B. Hopper: Transforming a checkered past

From Joe B. Hopper's resume, it's obvious he didn't have a clue about his future while in school or even after graduating. He served in the military, got an associate's degree in nursing science, then went after a BA in political science. He certainly had a mixed bag of credentials. On top of that, he has no business-related work history.

During career counseling, Joe decided he'd make excellent management material, specifically in operations management or benefits administration. Although his credentials suggest that he's weak management material—an effect created by his unrelated degrees, middling GPAs, and non-business-related job experience—Joe nonetheless crafted his resume to pitch his management potential. And he's done it well.

While Joe is currently employed in a supervisory capacity, his most substantial work history is with the military. So he listed that experi-

Joseph B. Hopper
1953 Barrie Street
Philomath, Georgia 39393
(404) 555-9876

OBJECTIVE

To obtain a position with a major corporation in a management training capacity.

EDUCATION

Georgia State University, Atlanta, GA, December 1994
Bachelor of Arts, Political Science, 3.0 Overall GPA

Philomath Community College, Philomath, GA, December 1992
Associates Degree, Nursing Sciences

MILITARY EXPERIENCE

7/87-7/91
U.S. Navy, Hospital Corpsman, E4

- Ultimately responsible for the direct supervision of 6-8 Naval Corpsmen throughout last 2 years of service.
- Appointed Head Company Corpsman by Platoon Director.
- Completed various courses in physical therapy, trauma, patient counseling and medical supervision. Finished first in the class in management training.
- Attended classes part-time during last 18 months of duty while full-time employed.

WORK HISTORY

12/92-present
Acme Fence and Roofing Company, Atlanta, GA
Crew Supervisor
Began as a general laborer and after 3 months was promoted to supervisor in charge of 5 to 8 man crews. Have recently begun to estimate jobs, which requires good problem-solving and negotiation skills and the ability to work well with people.

7/90-12/92
St. Mary's Hospital, Philomath, GA
Nurses' Aide
Temporary full-time employment while completing Associate's Degree. Volunteered for community service projects sponsored by St. Mary's to benefit geriatric patients. Attended seminars on Safety Training for Employees and Safety in the Workplace.

SPECIAL SKILLS AND ACHIEVEMENTS

Proficient in Lotus, WordPerfect, Microsoft, SPSS and DELTA DATA. Fluent in Spanish, partial fluency in German. Recipient of three community-sponsored scholarships.

ADDITIONAL INFORMATION

100% relocatable. Additional work history and references available on request.

ence first, even though he was discharged several years ago. This establishes a favorable pattern that repeats itself in his other job descriptions.

Joe has always been responsible for the activities of others or has achieved some sort of leadership role. He works hard for long hours, he deals well with all kinds of people, he's gained empathy from working with the elderly, and his trauma and nursing background have enhanced his problem-solving skills and his ability to work under pressure. His background may be scattered, but he's good management trainee material.

Let's not forget Joe's specialized training and bilingual ability. That makes him an extremely marketable manager trainee, if he's willing to relocate. And, of course, his resume attests to that fact.

So who cares if Joe B. Hopper has a liberal arts degree and no business background? He became someone as a *result* of getting his education. He transformed himself along the way into a future manager who's likely to be snapped up for a management training program.

Now it's your turn.

Charlie, Bill, Connie, Grady, and Joe are success stories. Warts and all, they managed to present themselves favorably enough on paper to land interviews and eventually launch real careers. And each one did it using a single page, with a little help from their cover letters.

Write your resume yourself, hone it to perfection, and the same kind of good things will happen to you.

9

Your Writing and Testing Skills

How Do They Measure Up?

Whenever I get a cover letter in which a candidate boasts about a particular skill or talent, I get out my imaginary magnifying glass. Actually, though, such candidates often make mistakes that virtually jump off the page. Take the young woman with an accounting degree who took pains to inform me that she was extremely detail-oriented. Each time she used the word "detail," however, she misspelled it as "detale."

Some people might think screening out a candidate for a misspelling is being picky, or "overly" picky. I disagree. It's a perfectly legitimate action when the quality she's trying to sell you is an eye for detail, and especially when that quality is integral to success in her chosen field. Each "detale" disproved the claim this candidate was making about herself.

Potentially, the interview process contains five opportunities for recruiters and/or employers to scrutinize your written communication skills: in the resume, cover letter, employment application, writing sample (required by many employers), and thank-you letter.

Since the previous two chapters brought you up to speed on resumes, we'll skip them here, and move on to that deceptively simple form: the employment application.

LOOKING AHEAD

Certain employers may also have you complete some paper-and-pencil tests. The idea is to gauge your honesty, psychological stability, and the like. Technically such tests don't fall under the umbrella of writing skills, but we'll cover them later in this chapter anyway. It's important for you to understand why these tests are given and to know how to take them.

So much of the following information is common sense, yet what I'm going to share with you is often reason for a candidate's rejection. Little things—like neatness and following simple directions—can be the things that ultimately stand between you and a job offer.

The employment application will become a permanent part of your employment file. This is the best reason to ensure that all of the information provided on it is honest and accurate. If you fudge on dates of employment or embellish job descriptions, your white lies are likely to be discovered in the reference check.

Read the directions carefully. Many applications start by asking you to *print* the information or have shaded areas that indicate *not* to print anything in those spaces. If you can't understand and follow these basic directions on the application, how will you follow directions on the job?

I won't use the old cliché "neatness counts." Let me put it this way: Neatness matters. If your handwriting is chicken scratch—or anything less than calligraphy-quality—take a little extra time to ensure that your words and numbers are legible. And if an employer mails you an application or gives you one to take home, don't fold, spindle, or mutilate the document. And, by all means, return it promptly to the employer!

TRAPS TO AVOID

Neatness, spelling, and grammar also matter. If you're a notoriously bad speller, get some help. And I don't mean the spell-check function on your word processor. It can't tell the difference between "not" and "now." (After all, they're both correctly spelled.) This is not a good thing when you hastily type sentences such as "I am not available for immediate hire."

Whats wrong with this sentence?

I recommend that you pick up four or five employment applications from different businesses. Why? Because the sampling will provide nearly every conceivable employment application question and give you opportunities for practice.

Fill out each application and recruit a literate friend to proofread your work. In particular, have the person note your misspellings and instances of bad grammar. Study the corrected applications and note any patterns in your mistakes. Then you can banish those bugaboos before filling out a real application.

The last crucial point about applications is thoroughness. Don't leave any blank spaces where answers are required. I've had clients rejected on that basis alone! Blame that old obsession with detail. If a job requires close attention and you skip over whole parts of your application, employers have the right to assume the worst about your skills in this area.

You're probably thinking that blanks should be acceptable for questions that don't apply to your situation. That's not quite true. In those cases, enter a dash or write "N/A" for "not applicable." That assures the employer that you have read and answered the question.

Blank spaces on your application can also create problems by allowing employers to draw their own conclusions about you. As you know so well by now, employers are conditioned to screen out candidates. Given almost any opportunity, they will draw a negative conclusion. The best example involves questions regarding criminal records. If you leave that space blank, the employer might well assume you do have a criminal past and that you chose not to make it a matter of record on the application.

The cover letter: Covering your bases

Some professionals say a cover letter isn't always necessary when mailing your resume, but I strongly suggest you include one. When properly done, it gives the employer an indication of your writing skills, conveys some personality, and gives you a vehicle to set yourself apart from your competition. Of course, if done improperly, that same cover letter could keep you *out* of a lot of interviews.

Having read thousands of letters and resumes over the years, I think I've seen it all. Sometimes I receive cover letters with no resumes, or worse yet, no phone numbers. I've gotten invitations to lunch via the cover letter. (Remember the fellow from an earlier chapter who invited me for coffee and doughnuts so we could get to know each other in a more "personable" setting?)

The cover letter is very handily named: It can be used to cover important points about yourself that might not be included in your resume. It's also a perfect way to cover any weaknesses or potential objections an employer might have regarding your credentials. So, use its

WAKE-UP CALL

Here's one for the books! I very recently received a cover letter that threatened me with a lawsuit for discrimination if I didn't grant the writer an interview! Not the best way to ingratiate yourself with a potential employer, to say the least. (I never contacted the individual, and I never was sued.)

name to remind you of its possible benefit … to cover the bases your resume doesn't.

Since the content of your cover letter hinges on your resume presentation and the specific position you're applying for, it's impossible for me to offer exact formats or models to follow. What I will do, however, is give you some helpful tips for making sure your cover letter is as good as it can be.

Ten tips for writing a winning cover letter

1. Keep it to one page and only about three or four paragraphs. You're writing an introduction, not a novel.

2. Have someone proofread it before you send it out. Don't rely on your computerized spell-checker. Correct any misspellings or typos. Use proper sentence structure.

3. The only handwritten item on your cover letter should be your signature. Don't make corrections or add any notes in the margins.

4. Don't design a "form" cover letter. Each letter should be written specifically for the company and position for which you're submitting your resume.

5. Make sure the letter has the correct layout and looks like a piece of business correspondence. Use proper format, margins, and line spacing.

6. Don't be cute. Don't use graphics, multiple typefaces, slang, or creative come-ons. Believe me, they don't work. Perhaps the one exception to this would be in the field of advertising, where creativity is a selling point.

7. Sell, sell, sell. If you know the job description, use at least one paragraph of your cover letter to highlight how your strengths match those required for success in the position.

8. Don't put limitations on yourself in the cover letter. *Don't indicate your salary requirements, even when specifically requested.* As an entry-level candidate, you have to be careful!

TRAPS TO AVOID

By indicating a specific dollar amount, you can price yourself out of an interview if your desired salary is higher than what the employer is prepared to pay.

Calling your salary requirement "negotiable" or "commensurate with what the market has to offer" is the best way to go. This approach doesn't screen you out. And it tells the employer that salary isn't the most important issue for you.

Avoid geographic limitations as well. I frequently get cover letters saying "I'd like to work within a 30-mile radius" or within a certain grouping of cities. The better tactic is to get the interview and hear the employer out first. You could be losing the opportunity of a lifetime. Would you really refuse a dream job because it's 45 miles away instead of 30? Setting such boundaries also signals a negative attitude about what price you're willing to pay in order to start your career.

9. Don't enclose a picture. You're looking for a career, not a modeling job. Sending a photograph of yourself is simply unprofessional.

10. Don't limit the times when potential employers can contact you. Perhaps you're working days and wish to be called at home in the evenings. While this is a reasonable request, most employers won't meet it. They have plenty of resumes and cover letters from people who can be reached during business hours. You can ask them to call you at work and be discreet, or give a daytime number connected to an answering machine. (Of course, you'll retrieve and return your messages as soon as possible.)

Required writing samples: Composition in real time

As a college graduate, you probably figured you'd never have to write another essay. In fact, you may not be off the hook just yet. Some corporations require a writing sample during the interview process. This is usually a sign (if it's not obvious already) that writing skills are part of the job for which you are interviewing.

The employer will usually give you a question or topic on which to write. In my clients' experience, the most typical essay topics are:

In one page or less, tell me why this company should hire you.

Or:

Why do you think you'd make a good (title of position you're interviewing for, e.g., underwriter, customer service trainee, sales rep, etc.)?

LOOKING AHEAD

Doing a corporate writing sample is like taking a blue-book exam—you have to compose on the spot, no take-home essays allowed. So it's smart to rehearse now. Sit down and answer those two questions based on the type of career you're seeking. Show your work to a friend or family member, get some feedback, and make any necessary adjustments to your content or writing style. Then, if the situation arises in an interview setting, you'll be better prepared for the challenge and more comfortable with your answers.

Not the stuff of creative writing, I agree. But if it's any consolation, your response will be read with as much interest as the latest novel by John Grisham.

While the questions are different, your answers should be similar. In both cases, you are being given an opportunity to sell yourself. And what you'll sell will be your strengths and aptitudes that tie into the job opening.

Thank-you letters: Gratitude plus stealth

The purpose of the thank-you letter isn't really to thank anyone. It's primarily a sales tool. Yes, you do want to begin or end the letter with a sentence indicating your appreciation of the interviewer's time. That's the "thanks" part. The other three or four paragraphs should be devoted to reselling your strengths and aptitudes and expressing your interest in the position and company.

Your note of thanks is also the place to overcome any objections that might have been raised in the interview. Study the following examples.

Sample thank-you #1: The value of speed

This is an actual letter from my files, faxed to the appropriate departmental vice president the day after the writer's job interview. The young woman knew that the job was a "fast hire" and wanted to ensure that her letter arrived before the decision was made—hence the fax. Also, because she had interviewed with two department managers as well as the VP, she faxed the letter to all three. The VP was the ultimate decision maker, but the other individuals had input, and she was wise not to ignore them.

Dear Mr. Rose,

Thank you for taking time out of your busy schedule to meet with me yesterday. I enjoyed talking with you and appreciated learning more about your sales audit opening.

From what I've learned, I believe The Limited provides exactly the type of work environment and career opportunity I've been seeking.

I also think I have what it takes to be successful in the position. Many of the job requirements are similar to those I have now. An eye for detail, problem-solving, working under stress, dealing with retail and mall management, and using Lotus are just a few examples. I also have a great work ethic and can learn quickly and easily. I'm sure I would catch on in no time flat.

I hope you'll give me every consideration when making your decision. I'll do my best to be the kind of employee you'd like to have working for you. Again, thanks for your time. I'll look forward to hearing from you next week.

Sample thank-you letter #2: The value of motivation

This young man had been told he was a great candidate but lacked a strong chemical engineering background needed for the position. In other words, he was rejected in the first interview.

However, his thank-you letter to the recruiter ultimately resulted in another interview for a different position at the same company. Despite rejection, his motivation was impressive enough to earn him another chance.

He sent this letter to the recruiter, with a copy to the sales manager—a good tactic. Recruiters have access to the openings in all departments of the company, whereas sales managers are concerned only with their own departmental openings.

Dear Mr. Stryker:

I've been doing a lot of interviewing lately, but none of the opportunities has excited me as much as the Sales Trainee position with BF Goodrich.

I learned on Friday that your Sales Manager is insisting on candidates with chemical engineering backgrounds. I want this opportunity. I know I have the sales ability, communication and people skills, a high degree of self-motivation, and the goal orientation necessary to succeed. All that's missing is the chemical background.

This is what I'd like to propose. If given the chance to get my foot in the door, I'll take the necessary classes on my time and at my expense. If that's the only thing standing in my way, I know I can learn quickly and easily and would be a productive member of your sales force in short order.

I really appreciated the chance to interview with you and look forward to when we can get together again.

Sample thank-you #3: The value of persistence

The scenario surrounding this letter is that the recruiter took a strong interest in the candidate and was very much an ally in the interviewing process. Hence, in the third paragraph, the writer is asking his assistance once again.

Manufacturing is a notoriously slow hire. It can easily take three months for industrial types to make a decision and extend an offer. That was the case here. This letter was sent as a memory jogger, a reminder that our candidate was still available and very much interested in the training program.

Dear Mr. George,

It's been a while since we've talked and I wanted to write and let you know how strong my interest remains in Campbells.

Being a Production Supervisor for Campbells is my idea of the perfect career. I'm confident I have what it takes to make a significant contribution to the company. I've got the leadership and management background, experience in manufacturing, excellent organizational skills, and am very motivated and goal-oriented. Not to mention the fact that I'd work my tail off for you!

Since I met with so many people, I'm hoping you'll let them all know just how much I want this opportunity. Any help you can give me would be greatly appreciated.

In closing, I just want to say one more thing. If Campbells gives me a chance at this opportunity, I will go the extra mile and do whatever it takes to succeed. I'll be looking forward to hearing from you soon.

The outcome of each interview will determine the form and content of your thank-you letter, the recipient(s), and the method of delivery.

If the department manager indicates in the interview that your chances aren't very good, send your thank-you letter to the human resource recruiter. Point out your assets once more and restate your interest in the company. Ask to be considered for future openings in areas better suited to your strengths. This letter can be snail-mailed. There's no urgency, so faxing or sending it by overnight delivery would be overkill.

By contrast, when you leave the first interview knowing you're under consideration for the position, send your thank-you to the department manager. If you have met with more than one hiring authority, send the letter to the person in the highest position and send a copy to the other managers. Or, send personalized letters to all the managers you spoke with. Either way is acceptable.

In some cases, expediency matters. If you suspect that the final decision will be made in a day or two, act fast. Respond by fax, overnight letter, e-mail, or even a telegram. Your initiative may provide just the edge you need. Otherwise, the U.S. mail will do just fine.

WAKE-UP CALL

One final, if unsurprising, point on thank-you letters: Do them right! Each letter should have the appearance of business correspondence (no cute notecards), be grammatically correct, and have no misspellings. In particular, make absolutely certain to spell the *name* of each recipient correctly and to use the correct title. That's easy to do if you ask for everyone's business card at the end of the interview.

Short, sweet, and accurate—three ideal attributes of a thank-you letter. Don't risk your chances with one that is badly written. Even if you've interviewed successfully, a sloppy thank-you letter could be the reason you are eliminated from consideration.

Getting put to the test

Just as you may never have to write a "why I want this job" essay, you may never need to take an employment-related test. Not all corporations administer them; the process is expensive and time-consuming. Also, the accuracy of the test assessment can be questionable, particularly for psychological tests.

Over the years, I've become familiar with dozens of different types of tests and testing methods. Some corporations develop their own tests and some employ companies or individuals who do the testing for them. These tests go by various names, too numerous to mention here. Instead of detailing them one by one, I'll provide the information you need to know about the different categories.

Aptitude tests

After years of PSATs, SATs, and the like, you shouldn't be flustered by aptitude tests. This type of test measures your abilities in math, reading comprehension, logic, flow charting, programming, or vocabulary. Employers in property casualty insurance, payroll and accounting services, and the actuarial industries are most likely to require aptitude tests. But be prepared for them whenever you interview for a position that requires number crunching, regardless of the industry.

Listen to the person giving instructions and read the instructions in the test booklet carefully. Follow directions. This goes for *all* tests *all* the time.

An aptitude test is usually timed and almost always monitored by someone from the human resources department.

DAMAGE CONTROL

Don't let the clock be your enemy in aptitude tests. It's not as important to complete *all* of the questions on the test as it is to correctly answer those you *do* complete.

Psychological tests

The goal of psychological tests is to determine personality type, sales aptitude, and leadership or management ability. From this type of test, the employer tries to learn whether you are more extroverted than introverted, a leader or follower, passive or active, and so on.

These tests have no right or wrong answers, in theory. For example, a multiple choice question might be, "Would you rather, a) take a walk in the woods, b) work on a jigsaw puzzle, or c) read a book to relax?" Or you might be asked if you are better suited to gardening or to being a mechanic. A third type of psychological query is: "When in a social setting such as a party, do you, a) feel more comfortable talking only with those people you know?, b) introduce yourself to others and make new acquaintances?, c) stay mostly to yourself, talking very little to anyone?, or d) usually make at least one new friend or business acquaintance?"

The results are supposed to give a better indication of whether your personality is suited to the opening. So if you're interviewing for

a sales position, you'd naturally select answers that indicate you're people-oriented, aggressive, assertive, active, and other positive sales qualities ... right?

Remember the suitability principle. You want a career that maximizes your strengths and avoids stressing your weaknesses. If you pretend to be someone or something you're not, you'll pay the price for it later.

Honesty tests

A small number of corporations once used polygraphs, or lie detector tests. (Their advocates called them "truth verifier" tests.) These involved hooking candidates up to physiological sensors while firing tough questions at them—enough to set a saint's heart to pounding. You'll be happy to know polygraphy testing is now illegal for employment purposes. However, you may be asked to take a psychological "profile" designed to measure your honesty and integrity.

I don't put a lot of stock in the results of these particular tests because you invariably have to lie on the test in order to pass it. You'll never fail an honesty test if you remember the following three rules when answering the questions.

Rule #1: Always be honest to a fault.

A sample question might be, "Have you ever taken anything from an employer without paying for it? If so, was the item valued at $1 or less, $1 to $10, $10 to $50, or more than $50?"

One of my clients answered this question honestly. He worked in a supermarket and during his lunch break he ate a cup of yogurt with every intention of paying for it by day's end. He forgot. On the test, he answered "yes" to this question and indicated $1.00 or less. He told the truth and failed the test.

So the question is, "If you found a quarter lying by the check-out counter, would you keep it or return it to the cashier?" *Of course* you'd return it to the cashier. Honesty to a fault.

Rule #2: Always turn in a friend, never turn in a relative.

Some questions probe for what you'd do if you saw someone else stealing, cheating, or breaking company policy. The guiding principle here is to turn in your co-worker but never rat on your mother.

If you saw a fellow employee take a candy bar without paying for it, would you report it to management? Absolutely yes. How about turning in your father if you learned he had embezzled $10,000 from the local bank? Absolutely not.

Here's another example. If you knew one of your employees had taken $10 from the safe, even though the employee indicated an intent to return the money, would you prosecute? The correct answer on an honesty test would be "yes."

If you answered that question logically, you'd probably say "no." A good manager would realize that prosecuting an employee over a $10 theft would cost the company more in legal fees and lost productivity than it could ever be worth. But in the skewed world of honesty tests, your "no" answer would be judged incorrect.

I didn't write these tests and I can't defend them. But I know enough about them to urge you *not* to use logic when answering such questions. Just remember and follow the rules.

Rule #3: Avoid guilt by association.

Some questions ask what percentage of your friends and relatives drink alcohol, use drugs, have criminal records, etc. Response is usually by multiple choice: 0 percent, 5–10 percent, 11–50 percent, 51–75 percent, or 76–100 percent. Always reply with zero or a very low percentage.

If you admit that 75 percent of your friends drink alcohol, the assumption is that you do, too. (Not an unfounded assumption, in fact.) If 25 percent of your pals have been arrested, employers will naturally think you associate with a less-than-reputable crowd.

GOOD NEWS

As an experienced test-taker, you probably know that the same questions may reappear three or more times with minor variations. That's to evaluate your consistency. Stay alert and don't be flustered. Rules #1, 2, and 3 apply to *all* honesty tests, no matter who designed them or is giving them. If you ever get stumped on a question, you need only apply the three basic rules in order to arrive at the correct answer!

Drug tests

Drug tests are a thing apart from paper-and-pencil tests, but this seems like the logical place to cover them.

Drug testing by employers is fairly common these days. Not many companies drug-test their employees at random, but quite a few require it of potential employees before extending an offer.

Be prepared to take a drug test as soon as you begin interviewing. Some employers test you on the first interview, some do the testing after the third interview. The point is that you won't have much advance notice, if any.

As you may have learned from Elaine's experience on a classic episode of *Seinfeld,* stay away from poppy seeds while you're interviewing. If you eat anything with poppy seeds as an ingredient within 24 hours of a drug test—muffins, pastries, bread, or your Aunt Laurie's prize-winning salad dressing—you risk testing "positive." And as with most medical tests, positive is not in your favor.

Your college career has given you plenty of writing and testing practice. By sharpening your skills in these areas, you vastly improve your chances of landing your first real job soon.

The face-to-face interview, though, is where the rubber really meets the road. Let's move on to that.

LOOKING AHEAD

Whenever you think you may be tested for drug use, take along any and all medications you are currently taking. It doesn't matter whether these are prescription drugs or over-the-counter items. Present them at the testing center and ask that they be listed in your file. If one of these medications happens to cause a false positive, you'll have documentation to back your claim. If you wait until you've learned that you failed the drug screen, however, it may be too late to produce evidence on your behalf.

10

The Interview

How Well Do You Communicate?

His mind was on vacation while his mouth worked overtime.

Glen was definitely a salesman. I knew it from the first time I spoke with him on the phone. He came across as very self-confident and goal-oriented, with an excellent command of language. He took the initiatives to keep our conversation going and was energetic and animated in his verbal presentation.

Glen's credentials weren't great, but he had a year of sales experience with two different companies since he graduated from college. Both were commission-only sales and he was generating an income. That's not an easy task for someone new to sales. The experience compensated for his 2.3 GPA, for his lack of extracurriculars, and the fact that he had made no contribution to his educational expenses. It was the pure profile of a campus party hound.

But given all those ingredients indicating Glen's clear potential as a sales trainee, I invited him in to meet with me.

During our first two-hour session I discovered quickly that, although Glen seemed like a good communicator over the phone, his communication skills were actually very, very poor.

First of all, he talked far too much and said far too little. I had a hard time getting a word in edgewise. And even though he monopolized the conversation, he wasn't saying much that was of any interest to me. By midinterview, my attention span had become very short. I was beginning to recall an old jazz tune, "Your Mind Is On Vacation But Your Mouth Is Working Overtime."

Classically egocentric, Glen focused on himself. He told me how great he was, how motivated, how goal-oriented, how successful he would be in sales. He never offered any proof of his assets or backup for his claims. He came across as all superficiality and no substance. Plus, he was so busy talking about himself that he didn't bother to ask any questions about me, my client companies, my business ... nothing.

Glen also talked too fast and frequently interrupted me. In general, he came across as a high-pressure hustler type. Not the required image for a salaried sales career.

Last but not least, Glen had an excuse for everything. Any query I made about the gaps in his background were met with defensive responses excusing his behavior. Bad grades? "It was the professor's fault. I don't know why, but he just had it in for me." Sporadic employment

during college? "I didn't have to work. My parents are pretty well off."
No extracurriculars? "I looked at a couple of different organizations,
but I couldn't see how they'd benefit me."

As the interview drew to a close, it dawned on me that Glen probably talked his way out of a lot of offers!

Glen was an extreme case, but lots of college graduates have no idea that being a good communicator in an interview demands much more than stringing words into sentences. Whether you talk too much or too little (a separate problem), you must focus on *what* you say and also on *how* you say it. Beyond that, effective communication also calls for initiative, some research, and the ability to ask good questions.

No matter how wonderful your credentials might be, no matter how good your image is, you'll never get an offer if you can't communicate well when it really counts—in an interview.

What you say: Content and substance

Your verbal presentation should be like your thank-you letters: short, sweet, and succinct. If you're flowery, elaborate, and take too long to make your point, you'll lose the attention of the interviewer. When you make someone sift through endless conversation to find the answers they're looking for, they'll quickly tune out altogether. No one wants to work that hard to learn what they need to know about you.

What exactly do I mean? Look at this example:

Interviewer: Why did you select the college you attended?

Ms. X: I looked at quite a few colleges in the Midwest that were highly ranked in business education. After visiting the campuses and checking on tuition assistance, I narrowed it down to three schools: the University of Michigan, Penn State, and Miami of Ohio. The three campuses were quite different in size and setting, so it wasn't an easy choice. I ultimately decided on Miami of Ohio because of its business curriculum, affordability, and easy access to three major market cities.

The answer to the key question is the very last sentence in the paragraph. If you consistently communicate as Ms. X does—and most college graduates of both sexes do—by midinterview recruiters and employers will have wearied of your ramblings. They will not hear what they need to hear in order to make a hiring decision.

The right way to respond is:

Interviewer: Why did you select the college you attended?

Mr. Y: I chose Miami of Ohio for its highly ranked business curriculum, its affordability, and its easy access to three major market cities. I checked out quite a few schools in the Midwest but applied only to Miami and two others.

This response supplies your answer immediately. No extraneous detail. It might even provoke the employer's curiosity about your other two college choices and prompt him to ask another question. It sets the stage for a more "conversational" interview..

Here's rule #1a: If you find yourself getting off the subject or getting into too much detail, stop talking.

Communicating is also about listening.

Another important tip for becoming a good interviewing conversationalist is to learn to listen, to the interviewers and to yourself.

Listen carefully to interviewers' questions and comments. Then, as the first words out of your mouth tell them what they need to know, listen to what you're saying. Is it to the point? Are you overelaborating or going on a tangent?

Better listeners simply make better communicators. And that's not all. By expounding too much on any given question, you close the door on further conversation. Eliminate the detail, or most of it. Be concise. You'll know if your responses are of interest because employers will take the initiative to ask for details. This process is called give-and-take. It works very well in keeping conversations and interviews flowing right along.

Give explanations, not excuses.

Too many college grads create a giant pitfall for themselves in interviews: They make excuses for the negatives about their backgrounds and credentials instead of offering explanations. It's a great way to come across as immature and whiny. And, it's a surefire way to eliminate yourself from consideration for just about any good job.

Through the years I've encountered few, if any, college grads with flawless credentials. Because a below-average GPA is the most common negative I encounter, let's use it as an example.

If your transcripts are loaded with failures or withdrawals and your GPA is lower than 2.8, you may be in for a surprise. Some employers aren't very forgiving of transcripts like this. Others are more accepting of a few bad grades and a lower GPA, but very few will let it slide without hearing your explanation.

You cannot excuse your grades by blaming someone else. You just can't. Employers draw the conclusion that if you did poorly or failed in the classroom and blamed it on the professor, you're likely to blame the employer if you are having difficulty in the training program. They'll also think that if you weren't getting enough attention in a big class, you'll expect a lot more attention as a trainee than they're prepared to give you.

Real explanations for real situations

Accept responsibility for your grades and any withdrawals you may have taken. After all, whose name is at the top of your transcript?

Instead of making excuses, consider some of the following as possible explanations:

- Perhaps you overloaded on semester hours.

- Maybe you had to work overtime in your job, and if you were paying your own tuition, employment took precedence.

- Maybe you were simply struggling with the coursework.

- If you were active in extracurriculars and held down a job, you might have spread yourself a little too thin.

On the other side of the coin, always point out when you *successfully repeated* a course that you dropped or failed the first time. That's a real plus.

Whatever your reasons for the gaps in your background, be honest and up-front. Your "no excuses" approach telegraphs a batch of positive messages: you have a good work ethic, are highly motivated, a team player, mature, responsible—all those wonderful things employers love to find in a candidate.

Here's another residual benefit of explaining rather than excusing a negative: It's an opportunity to soft-sell a positive about yourself.

Comb your Personal Inventory. List the negatives in your background and practice explaining them to your interviewer. The following checklist will help.

The five most common negatives and how to turn them around

Chances are you have at least one of the following negatives in your background. Because these five are the most common red flags, it's a sure bet that employers will want you to explain them. Prepare by asking yourself the questions I've outlined. They'll help you arrive at an explanation—not an excuse—that suits your situation.

Red flag #1: Gaps in employment

- Did you temporarily take time off to handle a heavier course load than usual?
- Did you take time off due to an illness, either yours or a family member's?
- Did you take time off to get more actively involved in one of your extracurriculars?
- Did you take time off to focus on studies in order to improve your grade point average?
- Did you work hard and save enough money to afford you the luxury of taking a vacation, either stateside or abroad?
- Did you take time off to research and prepare for your job search after graduating?

Red flag #2: Lack of involvement in campus-related extracurriculars

- Did you load up on classes to graduate on or ahead of schedule?
- Did you spend so many hours on the job that you were unable to devote the time to be actively involved?
- Did you instead devote that time to community service or tutoring?
- Do you have a hobby or other personal interest that consumes your spare time, e.g., karate, dance, community theater, etc.?

Red flag #3: Taking too long to graduate

- Did an illness, accident, or other extenuating circumstance cause you to take a semester or two off?

- Did you work full-time (or close to it) in order to pay your own way?
- Did you move to another city or state and experience an educational setback in the transition and transfer of colleges?
- Were you responsible for a family or the caretaking of your own children?
- Were you a member of the military or active in the reserves?
- Did you pursue a double major or dual degree?

Red flag #4: Changing your major more than once

- If you struggled with the coursework, did you seek out counseling from your advisor before making the change?
- Did you transfer colleges due to relocation and find the new college didn't offer the same curriculum?
- Did you get involved in an internship or professional organization that shed new light on the direction of your education?
- When you changed majors, did you choose another that best utilized and incorporated the courses you had already completed?
- Did you start out in a particular major to follow in the career footsteps of a parent or family member, and then realize you were not cut from the same cloth? (Believe it or not, I see a lot of second- and third-generation professionals grappling with this situation. Just because your grandfather and mother were successful civil engineers doesn't mean you'll be happy in that field, no matter how they may push you to pursue it.)
- Did you pursue a specific degree in order to contribute to a family-owned business and later discover your interests were in other areas?

Red flag #5: Transferring colleges

- Did you make the change due to relocation?
- Did you transfer to a more affordable college due to financial hardship?
- Did you transfer to a better or more highly regarded university?
- Did you transfer in order to have access to specialized training or education?
- Did you transfer to accommodate your employment or future career?
- Were you in the military and moved from base to base?

How you say it: Clarity and style

As I said earlier, *how* you communicate is as important as *what* you communicate. I find a lot of my clients are poor communicators not because they have little to say, but because they don't say it well.

Start by speaking clearly and enunciating your words. One particularly grating example of poor speech involves dropping the endings from your words: "What I'm sayin' is, I'm thinkin' about workin' in com-

LOOKING AHEAD

You don't need to shout during an interview, but here's the best reason not to mumble: If an interviewer has to ask you to repeat yourself at any time during the interview, *you may well have blown it*. Obviously that particular line of answer is important or the interviewer wouldn't press you on it. But how many times previously did the interviewer *not* hear you clearly and just not bother to ask you to repeat yourself?

munications an' doin' somethin' interestin' in that field." If you want to be a professional—in communications or anything else—you have to communicate in a professional manner.

Another issue to consider is volume. Speak up! When people are nervous or intimidated, they sometimes speak too softly from lack of self-assurance.

Grammar and word choice also matter. Avoid slang and use proper English. But don't go too far in the other direction. As I discussed earlier, I've seen too many clients try to raise the level of their discourse with large or infrequently used words that they would never use in everyday talk. They mispronounce these words and/or use them out of context. Go by this rule: *If it feels awkward to you, it will sound awkward to the employer.*

Last but not least, don't be afraid to show some expression and animation in your voice. Be aware that if you're feeling a bit nervous or intimidated, your speech patterns may change. You may unwittingly fall into a monotone delivery—the kiss of death. Enhance your personal presentation by allowing your enthusiasm and energy to shine through.

If you have weaknesses in any of these areas, it's a good idea to start working on them in noninterview situations. Ask your friends and family to point out your foibles—lazy speech, the overuse of slang, or whatever—as they occur in daily conversation. Being aware of the problem is half of the solution. The other half is working toward improvement.

Ask good questions to keep the interview moving.

Asking good questions doesn't happen by accident. Such questions are planned. And the more you know about the company, industry, and job description, the better and more relevant your questions will be.

Always remember that an interview is an exchange of information, a conversation. You and the employer have the same right to ask questions of each other and learn as much as possible about each other before deciding on a match.

In fact, asking questions is an excellent way for you to gain control in an interview, especially if it's a question to which you already know the answer. Use it to lead the interviewer into specific areas of conversation in order to sell your related strengths or simply to discuss subjects you feel most comfortable talking about.

There are specific areas in which you'll want to focus your questions. I'll give you some sample questions in each area, but I encourage you to come up with some of your own.

Good questions to ask about training

It makes sense to me that if you're interviewing for a training program, you want to know what it's all about in order to make an educated, informed career decision. There's no better time than the interview to find out what you need to know.

1. Could you tell me a little about your training program?
2. What qualities do you look for in a claims adjuster (*name of any occupation*) trainee?
3. How long does it usually take a trainee to complete the program?
4. What are some of the career paths others have followed as a result of going through this training program?
5. What's the typical timeframe for advancement out of training for the average candidate? How about an above-average candidate?
6. How does your training compare to that of other companies within your industry?
7. What are your expectations for a new trainee?
8. What kind of additional studies would you recommend that trainees pursue in their own time in order to prepare themselves for a career in this field?
9. How can I, as a trainee, make a contribution to this organization?
10. In the past, if a trainee didn't succeed in this position, what was usually missing?
11. What do you view as critical areas of development for a trainee?
12. How are your trainees evaluated and promoted?
13. Could you describe a typical first-year assignment?
14. Once training is completed, does the company promote further education and/or ongoing training in specialized fields?

Good questions to ask about long-term growth potential

Employers don't take chances on entry-level candidates; they take risks. Turning trainees into productive employees does cost a bundle in time and money, and the risk is high. With no past experience, there's no guarantee the individual will succeed.

Given this considerable investment, companies look for reassurance that you intend to stick around long enough to give them a return on their investment. That's why asking questions and making comments about long-term growth is reassuring to them.

1. If I put forth my best effort, where can I find myself in this company five years down the line?

2. What are the opportunities for professional growth within this organization?

3. Once I've completed training and my first management assignment, what types of ongoing education are provided in order to foster my upward mobility?

4. I've interviewed for a lot of jobs. I'm not interested in a job. I'm interested in a career offering opportunities for growth and advancement based on my contribution to the company. Is that what you have to offer?

5. What are your company's plans for future growth and development?

6. Is it your company's policy to promote from within? If I invest myself and work hard, I want to know there will be positions for me to grow into within the next three to five years.

7. At what point will I have some responsibility that is clearly my own and be given an opportunity to be evaluated on how well I handle it?

The fine art of using "in your opinion" questions

"In your opinion" questions are great in interviews for lots of reasons. Primarily, people in professional capacities usually like to talk about themselves and how they got where they are. So asking the right questions will almost guarantee a conversational, memorable interview rather than a cut-and-dried, question-and-answer session.

Also, these types of questions can be used over and over again. If you have an all-day interview and know you'll be interviewing with five people in succession, these questions can be asked of each person in each interview. It takes some heat off you when preparing for the interview. You still have to come up with a list of good questions, but you won't need as many. You might say recycling works as well with questions as it does with the environment.

Finally, "in your opinion" questions provide a great deal of insight you wouldn't ordinarily get in an interview. For example, you can inquire of the first interviewer: "When you went through training, what did you consider the most challenging aspect of the program?" When you get the response, follow it with "How did you handle that?" or "How did you overcome the problem?"

Now, think about it. If you followed that line of questioning with five different managers, you'd get five different answers. When you ask the follow-up question, it'll give you the ammunition you need to do better in each successive interview because of the insight and knowledge you've gained. Not only that, you'll be armed with more substantial information on which to base your career decision and will be better able to determine if you are a good match for that particular career.

TRAPS TO AVOID

In interviews, don't make your questioning too personal. Keep the questions relative to the company, job description, and industry. A lot of graduates I've represented over the years seem to think a personal conversation with the interviewer is beneficial to them. It's not. Read the following anecdotes to see why.

Don earned his tuition working as a blackjack dealer in Atlantic City. In his own opinion, he did well in interviews. That, he told me, was because he and the potential employers had spent so much time talking about gaming, casinos, and the like.

However, Don couldn't understand why he wasn't getting called back for second interviews. His subject matter made for interesting conversation, no doubt. But he didn't learn what he needed to know about potential employers, and worse yet, he took little or no initiative to sell his strengths.

Another trap you'll want to avoid is sports talk. Maybe you were a college athlete and you discover that your interviewer was too. Suddenly, you forget all about the company, the position, and how you might fit in. All of a sudden your interviewing hour is up and all you've discussed is the Big Ten.

Bottom line: Answer the interviewer's personal questions, but be brief. And be ready to move on to a question of your own that will get you back on the interviewing track.

Excellent examples of "in your opinion" questions

Try these in any interview and you can hardly go wrong:

1. Is this the same training program you went through? What did you find most challenging? How did you handle the challenge?

2. What do you think it takes to succeed in this position?

3. In your opinion, what has kept your company successful during this most recent recession?

4. What industry-wide trends do you feel are likely to affect your company?

5. What do you think makes your company different from your competition?

6. How would you describe your company's personality and management style?

7. What prompted your initial interest in this company? In other words, why did you want to come to work here?

8. What are some of the most challenging aspects of being a (*title of position*)?

9. What do you like most about working for this company? What do you like least?

10. How long have you been with the company and can you tell me a little about how you got to where you are today?

11. How were you recruited for your position with this company? What do you think you had that made them want to hire you?

12. Generally speaking, what do people find most interesting about their work in this field?

13. In your opinion, what kind of people generally succeed at this position and what strengths do they have in common?

14. Since you've grown into management with this company, it's clear you've been successful. What did you do differently from others that helped you to get where you are today?

15. What do you like most about this company? Where would you like to see some improvement, if any?

16. You've come this far with the company. Where do you think you'll be five years from now?

17. In your opinion, what are your company's greatest strengths? What do you think its weaknesses are?

Questions that show you care

Always remember that employers seek candidates with a keen interest in the industry, company, and the specific job opening at hand. Most managers employed by Fortune 500s think they work for the best company in their respective industry. They want to recruit like-minded people.

Part of your display of enthusiasm will stem from your research. The more you know about Company X, the more impressed your interviewer will be. So do your homework. Go to the library. Talk to people in the industry. Read *The Wall Street Journal, Forbes, Fortune,* and other business periodicals.

You should learn enough about a company or industry to ask at least six good questions that are highly specific. How specific? Note the

GOOD NEWS

How do you send the message that you're excited by the prospect of going to work for Company X? You don't need to get out your old cheerleading pom-poms or act bubbly if that's not your style. You'll convey plenty by your attitude and by the kinds of questions you ask.

following examples based on information from sources like the ones I just listed.

1. I noticed Campbell's is ranked 85th in sales in this year's issue of *Fortune's Industrial 500*. Yet in profits, you rank 38th among the top 500 manufacturers. To what factors do you attribute that high rate of profitability?

2. During this recent recession, The Limited has grown consistently in size and profitability while a lot of other retailers are closing their doors. To what do you attribute that growth in this economic climate?

3. I read a newspaper article recently that indicated Fifth Third Bancorp is ranked the nation's strongest and best-run bank among 219 publicly traded U.S. banks. It went on to say yours is also one of the most profitable. In light of this most recent recession and the restructuring of the banking industry, how do you account for such success?

Ask this type of question in addition to more general ones. Have six of these prepared, but don't worry if you don't get to ask them all. Even if you bring up only two, that's two more than most of your competition will. Which ones to ask will be determined by the conversational flow.

Obviously, you'll need to prepare all your questions prior to each interview. And don't rely solely on any I've listed here. Give the matter some thought. What do you really want to know about this position? This company? This industry?

If your questions are good and show depth of thought, I guarantee you will be received as a much more professional and mature candidate than your competition. And in a niche market, anything you can do to set yourself apart will increase and improve your chances of securing an offer.

11

Your Interviewing Skills

Ten Tips for Improvement

"I couldn't believe Kerry was the same person I had 'met' by phone."

As Kerry introduced herself on the phone, she seemed like the kind of person who makes others feel like lazy slugs. She had attended a top university and earned two degrees in four years and one semester. One was a BA in Political Science, the other a BS in Economics. Not the easiest majors.

Her grade point averages in both degrees were above 3.7. These were particularly impressive considering that Kerry had worked part-time while carrying all those credit hours. On top of that, she was president of her sorority, held offices in other campus organizations, and was active in community service projects.

Kerry had been out of college for almost a year when I first spoke with her. She was working full time as a sales associate in an upscale department store while conducting her career search. She was marketing herself in the banking industry, hoping to land a position in financial analysis.

After graduation, Kerry had landed quite a few interviews with some very high-profile corporations. That didn't surprise me, given her exceptional resume and credentials. But, given how well she came across in our phone interview, I was surprised to learn that she never made it to any follow-up interviews. I couldn't imagine a more perfect candidate. Naturally, I was eager to meet with her.

When she arrived for our interview, I spotted the discrepancy at once. Kerry came across as painfully shy and withdrawn. Her voice cracked when she talked and her palms were sweating profusely. She couldn't maintain eye contact and was visibly shaking, lips quivering and hands trembling.

Kerry was proof positive that while good credentials may open a lot of interviewing doors, they won't get you the job if you don't know how to interview well. It's another example of my theory that people hire people, not degrees and GPAs.

In short: The best credentials don't always land the offer. The person who interviews best usually gets the job!

I'm going to share some practical interviewing tips with you and show you how taking a little initiative will turn you into a more dynamic interviewer. No matter how good your interviewing skills might be, I guarantee at chapter's end they will be even better! In fact, if Kerry had this list before I met her, she probably never would have needed my help.

Interview tip #1: Set yourself apart from the competition.

When you're trying to land your first (or even second) career job out of college, you will face a much more competitive market than what you'd face with five to fifteen years of experience. On the surface, you and your competition are all offering the employer the same things. We've reviewed them before. You're all in the same age group; have degrees but little, if any, related experience; have extracurricular activities, and so on, and so on.

That's why the interview is such an important arena for setting yourself apart from the competition. If you talk about work experiences instead of classroom experiences ... if you dress well, carry yourself well, and communicate well ... if you're well prepared with smart questions and thoughtful answers ... you can and will distinguish yourself.

GOOD NEWS

If you take the initiative to follow even *some* of my suggestions, you will stand out among your competition in each and every interview! And, you will materially improve your chances of landing a career job in as little as six weeks.

Interview tip #2: Be prepared in case the interviewer can't interview.

Generally, your first interview is with someone in human resources, most likely a person with a degree in Human Resource Management, Personnel Management, or Psychology. They've been trained and educated in the interview process. They interview daily and know what kinds of questions to ask and what kinds of answers to look for.

The human resource interview is the screening interview. If you do well enough there, you get passed on to the department manager who, in most cases, is the ultimate hiring authority.

Unfortunately, department managers aren't always good interviewers. They may have degrees in accounting, engineering, biology, or no degree at all. In many cases, department managers have had no formal training in the art of conducting a thorough interview. Some companies do provide interview training for their management staff, but when managers don't conduct interviews regularly, their skills can be less than the best. In fact, most department managers conduct interviews only a few times a year.

Furthermore, your interviewer's primary function is to run the department. An interview is a necessary inconvenience, an interruption of the normal flow of work. The manager is very likely to be preoccupied with production, budgets, the day's latest crisis, looming deadlines, personnel problems, or personal problems.

So if your fate is in the hands of a person who seems distracted, don't take it personally. Maintain your interviewing focus. You're there to sell yourself, to ask good questions, and to give the best possible answers to the questions asked of you.

What if you're not being *asked* the right questions? You still have to provide the information that is needed to make the hiring decision. Take the initiative to converse. Make a comment that sells one of your strengths. Fill an awkward pause with one of your well-prepared questions. Any and all of those tactics will put the interview on course. Don't try to run the show, but don't be afraid to fill any gaps in the conversation. After all, you've researched the company and you're thoroughly prepared.

Interview tip #3: Take charge of the interview.

The interview will always "belong" to the interviewer. It's that person's company, opening, office, and interviewing style. You'll have to adapt, but you don't have to roll over and play dead.

Typical college graduates allow themselves to be led through interviews. They wait for the question, give the answer, and wait for the next question. It's like an excruciating game of tennis.

You do have rights in an interview, and you need to learn how to exercise them. Remember, an interview is an exchange of information. You are there to explore as much as you can about the employer, just as they want to learn about you.

As you learned in Chapter 10, the amount of product knowledge you possess and the types of questions you ask will arm you with the ability to take charge if needed. A thoughtful question can be one of your most effective interviewing tools. It's as simple as the following example: You're interviewing for a position as a claims adjuster trainee. Through research, you've discovered that successful claims adjusters are usually detail-oriented, have good organizational and planning skills, can com-

FIXING MISTAKES

At the end of most interviews, the employer invariably asks if there are any questions. The reason most interviews finish that way is because the graduates never took the initiative to ask any questions *during* the interview! Don't make that mistake.

municate well, are able to get along well with people, have the ability to work well under pressure, and are multitask-oriented.

If you possess any of those qualities, you ask the employer the question, "What strengths do you feel are necessary for a person to succeed in the claims field?" Almost certainly the response will include one or more strengths you possess. You then go on to indicate which of those qualities you've developed over the years and provide the proof in your explanation.

Sure, you knew the answer to the question before you asked it. But *by asking it,* you open the door to sell a strength or to reinforce your interest in the company and your suitability to the position.

A well-posed question can also move you and the interviewer to an area of discussion you can't afford to overlook. Or it can help you change the subject to one with which you're more comfortable. You have the ability to take charge. You just have to learn to use it.

Interview tip #4: Correct misunderstandings and mistakes.

We've all heard ourselves say something that we immediately regret. I always ask my clients if they've ever said anything in an interview that *they* thought was really dumb. Invariably, they answer "yes."

But when I ask them what they did about it, most say "nothing." They just kept rolling along, and that remark they regretted so much continued to haunt them through the interview and beyond. In fact, instead of giving 100 percent of their energy to the rest of the interview, their mind remained stuck on that one bad answer. They regretted it and didn't know what to do about it.

You've probably been there. You've departed from an interview thinking it went smoothly "except for that one dumb remark I made." You thought about it all the way home. When your parents asked how the interview went, you replied: "Great, except for one really dumb answer I gave." When the rejection letter arrived a week or two later, you slapped your forehead and said: "I probably lost out because of that one stupid answer."

FIXING MISTAKES

Stop carrying all that garbage around with you. Get rid of it right away. When you blurt out an answer and it's not quite right, *you* know it immediately and usually so does the employer. So take the initiative to say something like, "Listen, that didn't come out quite right. Do you mind if I take another crack at my answer?"

Are they going to say "No, you can't!"? I don't think so. You have the opportunity to fix the problem, imagined or otherwise, right then and there, *if you ask for it!*

Instead of indicating a weakness on your part, this form of damage control bolsters your strengths. You're free to focus on giving your next best answer or asking your next best question. You're not using your mental energy to beat yourself up. In addition to correcting the misunderstanding, your action tells the employer you're a mature candidate. You're able to sit across from a stranger and say, "Hey, I made a mistake. I'd like to take the initiative to correct it." That's something the majority of recent graduates do not do.

You also get practice in sharpening your communication skills. If you're the type of person who rambles on and yet says too little, this is a great way of correcting the problem. Suppose you're answering a question and realize it's taking you forever to get to the point. Stop in midsentence if necessary and use one of these magic phrases:

"I'm getting a little off-track here. Would you mind if I start over?"
"Wow, it sounds like I'm giving you my life story. I'd like to start over and be more to the point."

Not only do you correct the mistake, but by listening to yourself, you'll eventually work the "rambling kinks" out of your conversation.

Interview tip #5: Ask for an explanation of anything you don't understand.

The workplace is a world unto itself, and industries often have their own jargon and catch phrases. So it's very possible that interviewers will use incomprehensible terminology or comment on subjects you're not familiar with.

If this happens at any time, take the initiative to ask for clarification. When the interviewer talks about programs, systems, or methods of operation you haven't been educated in, it's perfectly okay to say, "I'm not familiar with that. Could you explain it to me?"

Asking for help is far better than sitting across the desk and nodding your head in agreement when you don't have a clue what the interviewer is talking about. You don't have to pretend you know it all.

Some of my clients have worried that their willingness to say "I don't know" will be taken as a show of weakness. Not to worry. It's actually a display of maturity, strength, self-assuredness, and confidence on your part.

GOOD NEWS

Asking for details shows that you've been listening to what's been said, that it matters to you, and that you want to know more.

This is one tip that would have *really* helped Kerry. An interviewing flaw is anything about you that would detract from your performance in the interview. It could be nervousness, a cold, a speech impediment, the fact you're running late because of traffic, or a coffee stain on your shirt. If you have a flaw, inherent or otherwise, you need to address it *immediately* upon entering the interview.

Recent graduates and experienced people alike can become nervous and intimidated in an interview setting. That's nothing to be ashamed of. In fact, it's quite natural to be a little tense. But if your nervousness manifests itself in a physical way—heavy perspiration, shaking, a cracking voice, or the jitters—you can't pretend it doesn't exist. Yet that's what most people do. They expend a lot of energy trying to keep the employer from discovering their "flaw." By admitting to yourself and the interviewer that you're a little nervous, you take a great weight off your shoulders.

At the beginning of the interview when shaking the employer's hand and introducing yourself, simply say, "Good afternoon, I'm Kerry Allen and I'm really excited about this interview today. In fact, I'm pretty nervous and I hope you'll take that into consideration." Or: "Hi, I'm Kerry Allen. This interview means a great deal to me and I'm a little nervous. I hope you understand."

What's the employer going to say? "Leave at once! I don't interview nervous people!" Of course not. They've been on the other side of the interviewing desk and probably felt the same nervous feelings when they interviewed for their job. In almost every case, you'll tap into the employers' empathy. They understand; they've been there.

More importantly, admitting your interviewing flaw up front frees you to focus on the interview.

Probably my favorite story in this department comes from a past client of mine. Mark had a five-hour drive to get to an interview at 8:30 a.m. I suggested he depart the night before and stay in a hotel, but he chose to drive in the wee hours of the morning. Mark also didn't follow my suggestion to dress casually and change into his interviewing suit once he had arrived.

At 8 a.m. Mark phoned me in a panic, saying I had to cancel his interview. In his last few minutes of driving, he had spilled coffee on his shirt and tie. He had no change of clothes, and no stores were open at that hour where he could buy another shirt.

I told Mark he was foolish to pass up the opportunity because of a coffee stain. I suggested he treat it like an interviewing flaw, with words like: "Hi, I'm Mark DiBlasio and, as you can see, I had a little accident in the car on the way down here this morning. I sure didn't want this coffee stain to stand between me and this career opportunity and I hope you'll forgive my appearance. It's not typical of me." Of course the employer forgave him. Why wouldn't he? Mark had been driving since 3:30 in the morning.

As it turned out, Mark spent nearly the entire day at the company and was soon told he was their number one candidate. Ultimately, he won an offer. Walking away from the opportunity because of that little

WAKE-UP CALL

Honesty is also the best policy in other common interview-flaw situations:

Slight illness. Feeling a bit under the weather? Calling to reschedule an interview because you have a cold or other minor ailment won't win you points in the employer's eyes. It may raise doubts about your reliability and dependability. Better to keep the appointment, shake the employer's hand, and say something like this: "I'm Sam Pardoe and I'm really looking forward to this interview. Yesterday I seem to have caught that cold that's going around, but I didn't want it standing between me and this opportunity. I hope you'll understand."

Traffic woes. When you've been detained by traffic and are running late, that too can be held against you. First, make every attempt to telephone the employer to say you're on the way. Upon arrival, address the situation immediately. For example: "Good morning, I'm Jennifer Jackson. I have to tell you I'm a little tense and on edge from having been stuck in traffic. I sincerely apologize for being late, and in spite of the circumstances, I'm hoping you'll give me every consideration."

java splash could have cost him a terrific job. Sure, it's an off-the-wall example, but it really happened.

You never know what problem might crop up the day of your interview. But if something does arise, you can probably treat it as an interviewing flaw and salvage the interview. Address the problem up front, and then use your energy to interview to the best of your ability. In doing so, you will certainly set yourself apart from the competition.

Interview tip #7: Avoid negative feedback.

Are you a chronic naysayer? Are you likely to comment negatively about the company, the job you're interviewing for, your past employers, or your former professors? If so, putting a noose around your neck will save time. Why? Because any negative feedback kills your chances for an offer or even a second interview.

No job is going to be without its negatives. When you're in an interview, you can expect to hear about them. In fact, if the employer doesn't tell you what they are, I strongly suggest you ask.

Not very many employers paint a totally rosy picture. Actually, it's quite the opposite. Many employers will dwell on the negatives, and even embellish them, just to gauge your reaction. Perhaps you'll hear about the extra hours you may have to work, the number of times you may have to relocate, the initial salary that may be below your expec-

Keep in mind that negative feedback goes beyond the verbal. Good interviewers can pick up negative messages in your facial expressions and body language as well.

tations, the relative monotony of the job, or any of countless other aspects. Exaggerated or not, these all add up to an "attitude check."

Here's the trick: Tell them what they want to hear in the interview. Even if you foresee a problem on any particular issue, you can deal with it later.

Let's imagine a potential employer is saying you'll have to relocate to World's End, Wisconsin, where winter lasts eight months. You really don't want to relocate at all. Or maybe you're a summer person and want to relocate only to sunny places. If you say something to that effect in the interview, I guarantee you will not be asked back for another chance. (Same goes if you mutter "maybe," squirm a lot, and firmly cross your arms.)

Once you signal "no" or say it outright, the employer will decide you are the wrong person for the position. You no longer have a choice in the matter. In the interviewer's mind, the interview is over. *That's what negative feedback does. It ends the interview and takes away your right to choose.*

By responding in a positive fashion and saying you'll move anywhere to get your career started, however, you're telling them what they want to hear and maintaining your right to choose.

After you've heard the employer out, you may very well decide this is the chance of a lifetime. You give it some thought and decide a few years in Wisconsin is a small price to pay for a big opportunity. Or maybe you'll say "thanks, but no thanks."

Any negative response in the interview, however, would deny you the chance to make your own decision. The employer already made it for you and decided against you! It would be worse yet to discover later they don't even have a branch in Wisconsin. Employers have been known to test an entry-level candidate's attitude on the issue of relocation in this way.

Always respond positively to every negative issue the employer presents you with, regardless of what it is. It increases your chances of remaining in the running for the position, whether you ultimately decide you want it or not.

It is better to get an offer and reject it than to never get an offer at all. By being positive, you retain your powers of choice and control. By being negative, you give them away.

In an earlier chapter we discussed how negativity toward previous employers or educators also serves to eliminate you from consideration for a job. That never changes. No matter how much of a tyrant or ogre

LOOKING AHEAD

The time to digest the pros and cons of a less-than-ideal job offer is after it comes. Take a sheet of paper, fold it in half lengthwise and label one side "Whys?" and the other "Why Nots?" Then make your lists. You may have 20 reasons to accept an offer, but one burning reason to turn it down. That's just fine. That's the point of the exercise.

your boss or professor might have been, focus on the positive. Surely you learned *something* as a result of having been exposed to the person.

As an interviewer, my antenna goes up whenever I hear someone pinning blame on a previous employer or teacher. I assume that if I help get this candidate a job and it doesn't work out well, it will somehow be *my* fault. I don't need the aggravation.

Negative feedback is one of the best ways to get weeded out of consideration. Don't focus on the clouds; look for the silver linings.

Interview tip #8: Sell yourself!

Selling yourself is a deliberate act. The plain and simple fact is that if *you* don't do it, it won't get done. The importance of selling yourself in an interview has been a topic discussed throughout this book. We've covered what to sell about yourself, where to sell it, and to whom to sell it. Now, we're going to cover why, when, and how to sell yourself in an interview.

Let's back up a bit. There are basically two kinds of interviews, unstructured and structured. An unstructured interview is very conversational. By following some of the suggestions I've given in this book, you can almost always keep your interviews unstructured. In the unstructured interview you'll sell yourself from beginning to end, based on the information that comes up in the conversation. The employer will give you the time you need to explain and expand on your answers, and you'll use those opportunities to sell your relevant strengths.

The structured interview is more cut and dried. It's usually more formatted—the employer uses a list of preprinted questions, reads them in order, and makes notes along the way. This type of interview is more common among employers who aren't professional interviewers, and it's usually much less conversational. When interviewers don't give you a lot of room to sell yourself, don't force the issue. It's their interview and you'll have to adapt to their style.

If the interviewer hasn't given you a job description at this point, elicit one in order to sell your related strengths. Maybe you've done your homework and feel confident you know what the job is all about. That doesn't matter—request the job description anyway. Once

you've been told what you asked to hear, follow up with a comment like, "By virtue of that description, I feel confident I have the potential to do well in the position. Let me tell you why." You then proceed to sell yourself.

If the interviewer has given you a sufficient job description, don't ask again what it takes to be successful in the position. Instead, simply say, "I get the feeling we're winding down here. Before I leave, I want to tell you that I feel confident I have the potential to do well in this position, and I'd like to tell you why."

You then raise four or five of the job requirements that just happen to coincide with your strengths. Remember, you can't just rattle them off. As we discussed earlier, you have to follow each strength with an example of how you've proven yourself in the past. Backing the claims you make about yourself is what makes the sale successful. Otherwise, you're offering empty promises.

In structured and unstructured interviews alike, your task is to make a convincing connection between *your* strengths and *their* job description. You're the product and you're the salesperson. Take the initiative to sell yourself!

Interview tip #9: Ask for the job offer.

Kerry was well suited to every position for which she had interviewed. Her potential employers were all Fortune 100 companies, and she had a strong interest in each opportunity. Her obvious excitement about her prospects helped to fuel her natural nervousness during the interviews. Yet she never told any employer that she was interested in what they had to offer! Believe it or not, she didn't think it was right to be so bold!

There's a reason, a time, and a method involved in asking for the job. And it might surprise you to know that your real reason is *not* to get an offer.

In fact, your deeper purpose is to convey positive messages about yourself to the employer. By asking for the job you'll telegraph a strong sense of self-confidence, self-assuredness, motivation, and desire. It's the best way to let the employer know you're interested in what the company has to offer.

From experience, I'd estimate that fewer than one in ten interviewees actually ask for the job. That includes people with experience, who are much more likely to do it than recent college graduates. So simply by asking for the offer, you really stand out from your competition.

Asking for the job also distinguishes you from the competition. During counseling I always ask my clients if they have taken the initiative to ask for the job offer. Most haven't. Why not? Like Kerry, they say they didn't feel it was appropriate or they simply didn't feel comfortable doing it.

If you're a widget-maker with five years of experience who is interviewing with another widget manufacturer, you'll certainly say that you've done the job well for Company A and are confident you will do equally well for Company B. That's asking for the job. Unfortunately, it's a form of "asking" that doesn't arise with most recent college graduates, due to their lack of work experience.

When do you ask? Toward the end of the interview, as you might guess. Any sooner and you'll sound somewhat presumptuous. Gather as much information as possible to prepare for taking the plunge. Even if you interview with three people in succession at the same company on the same day, don't just ask your final contact or the person who seems highest on the decision-making ladder. Convey your interest to each and every interviewer!

Having covered *why* and *when,* let's talk about *how* to ask for the offer. Being subtle is the key here. You can't hit someone over the head by blurting out: "Can I have the job?" And phrases like "So, when can I start?" make you seem overly confident and cocky.

The subtlety comes in leading into the question with an assurance to the employer about your suitability. Let them know that the job description and responsibilities they've described are within your reach, that you feel confident you're equipped to handle the challenge. Basically, you're reassuring them about their decision to hire you.

The second key to your success is sincerity. The employer has to believe that what you're saying to them is true. You can't just mouth the words. A sincere request will go a lot farther in convincing the employer that you mean what you say.

Here are a few examples of appropriate ways to ask a potential employer for the job. Notice they're not all questions! There are literally hundreds of ways to communicate your desire. Read these over to get a general idea and then come up with a method that suits your style and personality.

Here are some effective ways to ask for the offer:

"Listen, Mr. Jones, I really like what you've shown me here today. I feel confident I'd do very well in this type of opportunity and I'd like to know what it takes to get on board."

"I've interviewed for a lot of jobs, but this is a career opportunity I feel I can sink my teeth into. I feel strongly that I have what it takes to succeed and would love an opportunity to work for your organization."

"By virtue of what I've learned here today, I feel I'm very well suited for this position. If given an opportunity, I think I could be an asset to the company."

"Before I leave today, I want to let you know I'm very excited at the prospect of becoming a trainee in this organization. My strengths are well suited to the job description, and I'm confident your investment in me would pay off in the long run."

"I hope your interest in me is equal to my interest in the company. From what I've learned here today, I'm confident I have the skills and potential necessary to succeed here."

"If the company is willing to invest in me, I'd work very hard to ensure your investment paid off in the long term. I think I have what it takes to succeed in the position and hope you'll give me every consideration when making your hiring decision."

You'll notice each question or statement in some way is accompanied by a reassurance of the candidate's ability to perform. That stroking is absolutely necessary when conveying your interest to the employer. It adds to the subtlety *and* the sincerity of the request.

Interview tip #9a: Don't take the first offer.

What happens if you've done a great job interviewing, have told the employer you're interested in the opportunity, and receive an offer in the first interview? *Don't accept it!*

Of course, not accepting an offer doesn't mean rejecting it outright. Don't turn the employer down. Instead, let them know you're flattered and/or excited about their decision to hire you. Say that because it's a decision sure to affect other people and areas in your life,

TRAPS TO AVOID

Whenever an employer offers you a job on the spot, I'd think twice about taking it. Most reputable firms like to select their potential employees carefully and cautiously. With most major corporations, multiple interviews and reference checks are a matter of course. There are exceptions, of course, but consider my warning. You don't want to jump into a situation you may regret.

you'd like to have a little time to respond with your final decision. A reasonable time frame is usually one or two business days. If you ask for more time, the employer might think you weren't very sincere in your request and then retract the offer.

If an offer is extended in the second or third interview, you can accept or decline on the spot because you've already had enough time to deliberate over your decision. You're not being hasty and you've had plenty of opportunity to weigh the facts.

One more point about asking for the offer. *Do it every time you interview, whether you want the job or not.* As I've often noted, it's better to get an offer and turn it down than to never get one at all. Pretend you have an "interviewing belt" and carve a new notch in it for every offer you get. The goal is to cut all the leather away. Getting the offer is the truest test of your interviewing skills.

By asking every time, you'll get much-needed interviewing practice and the chance to polish your skills in the process. Then, when you find the job you really want, you'll be better at the business of asking and more confident and believable in your presentation. Getting an offer is a marvelous confidence builder. It gives you a kind of halo that does wonders for the dynamics in subsequent interviews.

Interview tip #10: Close the sale.

The interview is ending. You've spent nearly an hour selling the employer on all the reasons why you're the right person for the opening. You now have one more job to do before you leave. You need to close the sale.

Many people claim to be able to sell, but without this crucial step their deal might very well slip through their fingers. No sale is complete without a close, and the same holds true in an interview.

In fact, the close might be the most important thing you do before walking out the door. It's a way of finding out how you did, what the competition is like, and when you'll be back. Most importantly, it's your last chance to overcome any objections the employer might have about hiring you. In addition, it's one more way of helping you stand out in the crowd.

At the end of every interview, take the initiative to learn where you stand in the employer's eyes.

The four keys to the close are:

1. Find out what your competition is like.

2. Find out if there are any objections or obstacles to overcome.

3. Ask if there's anything you can do to improve your chances.

4. Ask what the next step is.

Always close your interviews with questions regarding issues 1 and 4. Whether you refer to issues 2 and 3 depends entirely on the interviewer's response to the first question.

If I were you, I'd want to know how I did and where I stand among the competition. After all, you've gone through a lot and have invested a lot of time and energy to come this far. Don't you really want to know how you did?

Questions like, "How do I stack up against the competition?", "How did I do today?", "What's my competition like?", or "What do you think my chances are?" are all good ways to assess your standing. You may be surprised at how candid most employers are in their responses.

If you learn you're the number one candidate at this point, you're certainly not going to ask them if there are any objections or obstacles to overcome or what you can do to improve your chances. You'll move immediately to "What's the next step?" or "When can we get together again?"

More likely, you'll hear something like: "You did very well, but we're still interviewing candidates through the end of next week." Or: "You're one of the top three candidates thus far, but we're still in the process of conducting first interviews." Any answer from the employer along those lines should prompt you to close them on points 2 and 3.

When you ask if there's anything about your background that might prove to be an obstacle, they'll share their concerns with you and give you one last opportunity to provide an explanation or reassurance. This is the perfect opportunity for you to overcome any objections. It's also your last chance to fix any mistakes or correct any misunderstandings.

Let's say you ask the first question and the response is that there's another candidate who seems a bit more qualified. Don't tuck your tail between your legs and slink off. Find out what Numero Uno possesses that you don't. Yes, it's okay simply to say, "So what does the candidate have that I don't?" More often than you'd imagine, the employer's response might help you save the interview.

Here's a perfect example. Jennifer had a BS in Economics from Carnegie Mellon University. I sent her to interview for an internal audit position with a major bank. It was her second interview with them and she was very excited about the position and the company.

When Jennifer asked about the competition, she was told that her credentials were impressive but that another candidate was "a little more qualified." Naturally, she asked for a brief explanation.

The employer told her that the other candidate was a finance major with four accounting courses. Jennifer had only two such courses. Her immediate comeback was: "I want this opportunity, and if that's all that stands in my way, I'll take those two accounting courses at my own expense if you'll give me a chance at this."

Jennifer had absolutely nothing to lose. In fact, by asking those questions and responding as she did, she wowed the employer. And yes, they hired her over the candidate with the better credentials.

If you determine that you are not the top candidate and have dealt with the employer's objections, it's time to ask if there's anything you can do to improve your chances. What might help you move up a rung on the interviewing ladder?

You might learn that there *is* some action you can take, but the real purpose of this question is to convey strong self-motivation and determination. Frequently, the mere act of asking question 3 will advance you in the rankings.

Once you've asked questions 2 and 3, don't leave before inquiring about the next step in the interviewing process. When can you expect to hear from them? What kind of time frame are you looking at? When will a final decision be made? How many more candidates are left to interview? These are legitimate questions to which you should learn the answers. This is also the kind of information an employer usually doesn't give you unless you ask. So ask!

Politely request the interviewer's business card. Ask if it's acceptable to call them in a week or so to follow up. The business card is your insurance for the correct spelling of the interviewer's name, an exact title, and an address or fax number to which you can send your thank-you letter.

Before you leave, also shake the interviewer's hand, extend thanks for the time spent, and say that you'll be looking forward to meeting again. That's nothing more than common courtesy.

Well, that's it. You've made it through the first interview. At this point, your chances are much better for getting called back for a second interview.

Handling special interview situations

Your first interview is usually the most typical kind. It's usually face-to-face and conducted in an office. It has a specific purpose: to land a callback interview. That's an interview of a different kind.

There are other types of interviews as well. Perhaps you'll spend the day at a company and be asked to interview at a luncheon with a few managers or staff members. Or maybe you live thousands of miles from your prospective employer, in which case your first interview may take place by telephone.

Each of these situations has its own protocol. Familiarize yourself with the various possibilities and you'll be ready for almost anything.

The nuts and bolts of callback interviews

Callbacks instill hope and set your heart racing. What a great feeling to know you've made it to first base in the interviewing game! Be careful, though. You don't want to lose your edge or back off on selling your strengths because you're overly confident.

Sometimes an employer will say they'd like to see you for a third or fourth interview, just as a formality. Don't believe them. No interview is "just a formality." What you say and how you present yourself are still being evaluated.

A callback also means it's time to get down to the details of salary, benefits, and company policy. This is one time in particular that it pays to keep your attitude in check.

If the dollar amount is less than what you expected and your reaction and response indicate it's unsatisfactory, that could be enough to change the employer's mind about bringing you on board. Remember, any negative feedback ends the interview in the interviewer's mind.

An offer is an equation in which your starting salary is only one of many variables. (What are the others? See Chapter 15.) Remain positive, regardless of the dollar amount that is put on the table. Probe for specifics about benefits, savings plans, insurance, vacation policies, tuition refund, and the like. Often the whole package can be very appealing, even if the starting salary is a few thousand shy of your expectations.

The pitfalls and practices of luncheon interviews

Personally, I dislike luncheon interviews. They have been the demise of many of my candidates over the years. For that reason alone, I'll examine them microscopically and try to suggest some do's and don'ts for this delicate category of interviews.

Seven helpful hints for a lunch interview

1. Order what your interviewer does. Not the identical dish, necessarily. But if they order a sandwich, you order a sandwich. If they tuck into a three-course meal, you do the same. Why? Because it's difficult to interview effectively between bites. You find yourself trying to hurry up and chew and swallow so that you can answer the questions they've been asking while waiting for their tuna sandwich. If you're asked to order first, order something that's a one-course meal. It's better to let your interviewer talk with a full mouth than the other way around.

2. Order something easy to eat. Spaghetti, a meatball sandwich, or a hamburger with the works are sure to test your art of eating without making a mess!

3. Never season your food before tasting it. Yes, you read that correctly. An employer once gave me his assessment of a candidate of mine whom he had rejected. *The fact that this young man salted everything on his plate before tasting it became an issue in the evaluation and had a negative impact!* When I asked why, I was told that "seasoning one's food before tasting it indicates a personality type who's resistant to change and the incorporation of new ideas." A bizarre but true story!

4. Don't forget your manners. Of course you'll use the proper utensils and your napkin, and you'll avoid talking when you have a mouthful of food. But don't forget to be courteous to the servers and other restaurant employees. Don't order them around, complain to them, or treat them as though their main purpose is to satisfy your every whim. Say "please" and "thank you" to them.

   Karen was on her third interview for a marketing assistant position with a major hotel chain. She was born and raised in affluent surroundings and, during the course of the luncheon interview, treated the server as if he were her own personal attendant.

   She was interviewing for a position that would require a lot of business lunches and client entertaining. Because she would represent the hotel chain, her interviewers ruled her out because of her cavalier treatment of the restaurant personnel. They saw her attitude as potentially damaging to the hotel chain, since their business is all about providing courteous service to their customers.

5. Don't order any alcoholic beverages. Even if the employer orders a martini, do not follow suit.

6. Don't order the most expensive thing on the menu, and don't order more than you think you are able to eat. Waste not, want not.

7. Don't let down your guard. Some candidates have a tendency to get too comfortable or casual when the meeting takes place over a pita

WAKE-UP CALL

Many companies arrange for another trainee to take potential trainees out to lunch. If this happens to you, keep a special eye on yourself. You'll have much more in common with your lunchmate, and it'll be easier to let your guard down and let your interviewing skills slide.

If your quasi-interviewer is negative about the company or training program, don't get swallowed up in the bad vibes and don't contribute to them. This person may not be the hiring authority, but I guarantee they'll be asked the details of your luncheon conversation when they return to the office.

pocket. Even though you're eating, it's still an interview. The conversation may be less formal, but what you say and how you say it will still have an impact on whether or not you get hired.

The logistics of long-distance telephone interviews

For some people, like Kerry, telephone interviews are easier than in-person meetings. They can hide behind the phone. They don't have to worry about their posture or what they're wearing. They're more relaxed and comfortable with their conversation, and they come across as being more self confident.

But, of course, it's still an interview. You still need to sell the interviewer, not only on your strengths but on the prospect of inviting you for an in-person interview.

When you sense that the phone interview is winding down, take the initiative to tell your contact that you'll be happy to make the drive (or flight) in order to meet them in person. But don't ask if they'll pay for it! Most companies won't absorb the expense to fly in an entry-level candidate for a first interview. If you have to pay your way to get there, regard it as an investment. Then, if you do well enough to be invited back, the company might pay for the second trip and also reimburse you for the first. The same goes for car mileage, expenses, and overnight lodging.

The top ten real-world reasons for rejection

I often lecture on college campuses, where I'm usually given one hour to get my message across to the graduating seniors. Cramming 15 hours of counseling into 60 minutes isn't easy. So I decided to focus my talks on what I consider to be the most important factor in landing your first real job: the interview.

With the help of employers who regularly recruit college graduates, I've put together this list. These are the most common reasons for rejecting a candidate. This is real-world stuff. But, if you study this book, you can avoid hearing these reasons applied to you.

1. **Poor communication skills, both verbal and written**

   Too talkative

   Poor grammar and diction

   Sloppy resume and/or application

2. **Poor scholastic record**

   Low GPA with no valid explanation

   No extracurriculars

   Poor planning of college career

   Lack of focus and inability to define career goals

   Took too long to graduate

3. **Poor personal appearance**

4. **Lack of preparation for the interview**

    Knows nothing about the company/industry

    Asks no questions

5. **Lack of confidence and poise**

    Extreme nervousness

    Poor eye contact

    Introverted and unable to initiate conversation

6. **Unwillingness to relocate**

7. **Unrealistic expectations**

    Expects too much money

    Places too much emphasis on money/benefits

    Expects too much too soon and is unwilling to start at the bottom

8. **Lack of motivation**

    Inability to set goals and achieve them

    Shows no potential for, or interest in, advancement

9. **Lack of interviewing manners**

    Late for the interview

    Comes across as overbearing, cocky, too aggressive

    Interrupts the interviewer

    Appears disinterested and bored (no enthusiasm)

10. **Negative feedback**

    Makes derisive comments regarding past employers or educators

    Becomes defensive when asked about less than favorable aspects of background or experience

    Makes excuses instead of offering explanations

Study this list and study yourself. A little advance knowledge can be your saving grace. If you are familiar with all ten of the most common reasons for rejection and are prepared in advance of the interview, you won't get in your own way and you'll achieve the success you deserve.

I know I'm throwing an awful lot at you all at once to digest and put into practice. But, if you start using these tips to improve your interviewing techniques—even if only a few at a time—your odds of securing a second interview will increase significantly.

12

First Impressions

Putting Your Best Foot Forward

"I liked Steve's drive and commitment, but ..."

Steve was one of six children raised on a farm in Indiana. He was the first one in his family to complete a four-year degree—an accomplishment of which he was justifiably proud.

On the farm, Steve was always tearing apart the farm machinery and putting it back together. His father was quick to recognize Steve's mechanical ability, and began to rely on his help. By the time Steve was sixteen, he was handling most of the mechanical maintenance on the farm for his father.

Steve learned early on that he had a natural aptitude for working with machines and mechanical equipment. While still in high school, he decided to pursue a career in which he could use that talent. After completing his degree in mechanical engineering, he began interviewing for positions in machinery maintenance or design with equipment manufacturing companies. So far, no offers.

I was impressed when Steve called me. I liked his drive and commitment to his goal, and I appreciated the career focus he had at such an early age. He communicated very well over the phone and was confident in his potential. Based on our hour-long phone conversation, my first impression was that I liked him very much. I invited him in for an interview and he accepted.

When Steve showed up, I was shocked. He was wearing brown slacks and a short-sleeved shirt. No jacket. Once upon a time, the shirt had been white, but now it was a dingy yellow. The button-down collar was visibly frayed. His tie needed to be pressed, cleaned, or both. The slacks showed only the ghost of a crease. And it was hard to guess when his shoes had last seen a coat of polish. Weeks? Months? If I hadn't already gotten to know him over the phone, I guarantee that my opinion of him would have been entirely different.

The point I'm trying to make is that first impressions are very important in an interview. The clothes you wear *do* matter, but first impressions can also be based on what you say, how clean you are, the way you smell, your attitude, and the way you carry yourself.

Over the phone, my impression of Steve was based on what he said, as well as his attitude. It was very positive. So when he showed up for the interview dressed like a thrift-shop reject, I was more willing to overlook his flaws.

In psychology, that's referred to as a halo effect. When the first impression is a good one, it creates a positive halo.

If I had met Steve without benefit of our phone conversation or any previous introduction (which is the situation you'll encounter in *most* of your interviews!), my first impression would probably have been negative. And, fair or not, the impression would have been based solely on his sloppy appearance.

It takes only two or three minutes for the average person to form a first impression. If Steve had gone for a job interview dressed as he was, the employer probably would have formed a negative impression before Steve got one word out of his mouth. Because of his appearance, Steve was running the risk of creating a negative halo in every interview he went on!

If you interview with a human resource person, you'll probably have a little more time and a bit of leeway to make your first impression. That's because most of them have been educated on the what's and wherefore's of interviewing and are aware of the halo effect and its consequences. A department manager, however, doesn't usually have the background, and two to three minutes is all you'll get to form a positive impression. Make the most of it!

Interviewing is challenging enough. When you're operating under the positive halo of a good first impression, it's not as much of an uphill climb because the employer is already on your side! That's why this chapter is dedicated to putting your best foot forward at the start of every interview.

Steve was interviewing for positions in manufacturing. He'd already had an internship and some work history in a machine shop, and he knew that people who work on an equipment manufacturing floor don't usually wear three-piece suits to work.

Steve remembered hearing somewhere that a person should dress up to go job hunting. He assumed that meant simply wearing slacks instead of jeans, and a shirt and tie instead of a tee shirt. Steve didn't know that he needed advice on interviewing, so he never bothered to ask anyone. In any case, Steve's family wouldn't have been much help. His father, a second-generation farmer, was successfully self-employed and probably never had to interview in his life. So, based on his background and experience, Steve chose his job-seeking wardrobe out of ignorance. He thought he *was* dressed up for the interview. He simply wasn't aware of how important the "packaging" can be.

WAKE-UP CALL

Employers always assume you'll be wearing your very best for an interview. Don't let them down. If you're looking for a career, if you want to be a professional, then it stands to reason you should dress like one for your interview.

I always tell my clients they should be dressed as well as the interviewer, if not better. Dressing on the same professional level as the interviewer puts you on more of an equal footing in the interview. When you dress like a professional, you'll significantly increase the odds of being treated like one by the employer.

Dress for success in the interview. Once you land the job, dress according to whatever the company's standards and policy dictate. This is true of any type of career you might be interviewing for, whether it's in manufacturing, advertising, banking, nursing, biology, or civil engineering. Even if you know in advance of the interview that the company has a dress-down policy or atmosphere, you should still dress professionally *unless the interviewer has specifically told you to dress casually*.

I know I've been stressing the importance of standing out from your competition, but this does *not* apply to dressing for your interview. That day-glo tie or that hot pink dress may be your favorite, but leave them in the closet. Remember, you want to look like a professional, not a neon sign.

GOOD NEWS

Don't panic! You don't have to have a closet full of business suits, and you don't have to go spending a ton of money on a new wardrobe. One nicely tailored, navy blue suit will serve you well until you land an offer. If you're called back for a second interview, it's perfectly all right to wear the same suit. Since navy blue is the most widely accepted and most often worn color in interviews, the employer probably won't even notice. You can create the illusion of a new outfit simply by choosing a different shirt and tie or wearing a different blouse.

Helpful tips to create the best possible image

Most of the tips that follow are appropriate for both men and women. Some, however, are gender-specific. Let's start with the suit. As I've already mentioned, navy blue is the color most widely accepted for interviewing attire. Charcoal gray is another good color. So is dark brown. *Dark* is the secret. Dark colors project an air of authority. Wearing dark colors helps you create a positive image.

TRAPS TO AVOID

Always think twice about wearing black. Black is, of course, a dark color, but it's not always appropriate or flattering. Men, in particular, project a more somber image when wearing black. Another drawback to wearing black has to do with skin coloring. According to the skin tone charts used in the fashion industry, only those who have what's called a "winter" complexion can get away with wearing black. If you don't have the right skin tone, black will tend to drain the color from your face. So be very cautious about wearing black.

If you're considering buying a suit with a pattern, a subtle herringbone or toned-down pinstripe is an acceptable choice. Whatever you do, don't let the salesperson talk you into buying something trendy.

TRAPS TO AVOID

Women, in particular, have to worry about sales clerks who push the latest trends and fashions. Resist the temptation to buy something "cute" or "sexy." Stick to your guns. Remember the rule for interviewing: Be conservative, professional, and unobtrusive!

To achieve the conservative look, go for clean lines and no frills. No fluted waistlines, no large decorative buttons, no loud stripes, prints, or plaids, and no two-tone suits. Look for a knee-length skirt cut in straight lines. Pleated skirts are okay, but they don't hold up well in an all-day interview. They have a tendency to wrinkle much more easily than a straight or A-line skirt. Slacks are inappropriate for an interview for women. Don't even think of slacks when making your suit selection.

I recommend a single-breasted style for both men and women because it's more conservative. If you choose, you can go the double-breasted route if the style isn't too trendy.

Shoes are just as important as the rest of your outfit. If you're a man, you should always wear black shoes unless you've settled on a brown suit—in which case, you should wear brown shoes. The shoe style for both men and women should be simple and conservative. That means no fancy buckles, bows, or other ornaments. And by all means, don't forget to polish them! Believe it or not, I've actually had complaints from interviewers about candidates who didn't take the initiative to shine their shoes!

Women have the option of wearing color-coordinated shoes with their suit, whether navy, gray, black or dark brown. The heel of a woman's shoe should be no less than one inch and no more than two inches. Spike heels and sandals are out. So are flats. Flats are considered casual and shouldn't be worn when going for an interview.

The rules for socks and hosiery are simple. Men should select a sock color that matches the dominant color between their trousers and shoes. It's pretty easy. If you're wearing black shoes, wear black socks regardless of whether your suit is navy or charcoal gray. If you have a medical condition that requires you to wear white socks, slip on a pair of dark socks over the white ones for your interview.

Women should stick with a hosiery color that is skin-toned. Stay away from the fashion colors. Remember to tuck an extra pair of panty hose in your purse when going to an interview. That way, you'll be ready for a quick change in the ladies room in case you have an accidental snag. Simply stated, runs are tacky!

When it comes to shirts, the rules aren't as flexible for men as they are for women. Men should always wear a white shirt, solid white, not white-on-white. The two most acceptable styles for interviewing

FIXING MISTAKES

Here's a helpful tip for both men and women: *Don't* do your own washing and ironing! And, unless she's a pro, don't let your Mom do it either. Nothing looks worse with a good suit than a shirt with a collar that's rolled and wrinkled. Or worse yet, a white shirt or blouse that's beginning to look off-yellow. Send your shirts to the cleaners and have the collars heavily starched. Blouses, too, should be dry-cleaned or appropriately laundered and ironed.

are either a cotton oxford with a button-down collar or a plain white dress shirt. Whichever style you choose, make sure you always wear long sleeves.

Women have a lot more leeway in choosing a blouse. Although white, cream, ecru, or eggshell are the preferred colors, pastels are acceptable. The neckline should be simple and plain. Avoid lace, frills, embroidery, prints, stripes, florals, or bows. Don't get carried away with "style." And never, ever wear a V-neck blouse or any style that might display cleavage.

Choosing a necktie isn't always easy but if you follow the rules, you can't lose. Always select a color that *contrasts* with the color of the suit you've chosen to wear. *Don't* choose the identical color for your tie and suit. Clients who show up to interview in a navy suit and navy tie look like American Airlines pilots. Go for something traditional, not trendy. A bright, flashy, floral, or abstract tie will detract from the image you're trying to convey. Pick one with a rich color and a subtle print. Good colors are burgundy or wine, and the print could be a faint geometric pattern or a more traditional paisley. The epitome of the conservative look is, of course, the Ivy League diagonal stripe. Remember, your tie is not making the statement; you are.

The way you knot your tie is also important. I suggest the traditional four-in-hand knot. Depending on the fabric your tie is made of, a Windsor knot can make you look as though you have a grapefruit under your chin. By contrast, the four-in-hand is a small, tight knot that looks best with a traditional collar and is considered the standard knot for business wear. For easy, step-by-step instructions on tying a four-in-hand knot, follow the illustrations in Fig. 12-1.

When it comes to jewelry, one of everything is the rule. For men, that means one watch and one ring. Leave the earring at home. Don't wear tie bars, tie tacks, cuff links, gold chains, bracelets, lapel pins, or pocket handkerchiefs.

Women have a little more flexibility, but the one-of-everything rule still holds true. In fact, the less jewelry the better. Earrings should not hang below the lobe of your ear. Stud earrings or any plain earring no larger than a dime will work well. Bracelets and necklaces should be

Figure 12-1. Tying a four-in-hand knot

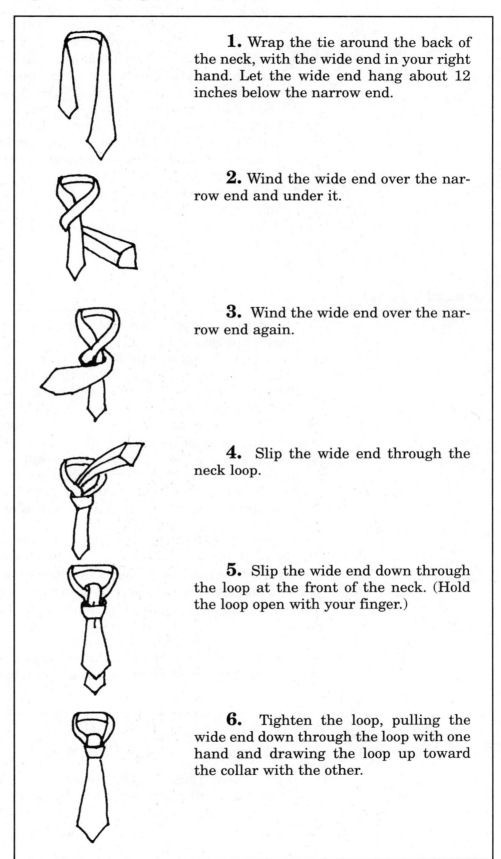

1. Wrap the tie around the back of the neck, with the wide end in your right hand. Let the wide end hang about 12 inches below the narrow end.

2. Wind the wide end over the narrow end and under it.

3. Wind the wide end over the narrow end again.

4. Slip the wide end through the neck loop.

5. Slip the wide end down through the loop at the front of the neck. (Hold the loop open with your finger.)

6. Tighten the loop, pulling the wide end down through the loop with one hand and drawing the loop up toward the collar with the other.

simple. Don't wear bracelets loaded down with charms or bangles that make noise with every movement of your arms. Try to color-coordinate your jewelry. Don't mix gold and silver. If the buttons on your suit are gold, your jewelry should coordinate in gold and vice versa. Aim for a look of classic restraint. And remember that less is better.

Luggage is the final item in your interviewing wardrobe. You don't need to carry a briefcase to an interview. A briefcase is overkill since you'll probably be carrying only a resume, a list of references, and a pen. A simple portfolio is all you'll need, and that goes for both genders. A leather-bound 9 × 12-inch folder-style notebook will hold everything you have very nicely. It's not cumbersome to carry and it provides easy access to its contents.

Women can certainly carry a purse in addition to the portfolio, but don't take a saddlebag stuffed with unnecessary junk. Your purse should be small and unobtrusive and should color-coordinate with your shoes.

Personal hygiene

It's hard to overemphasize the importance of being clean and neat whenever you go for an interview. Take a giant step toward a positive impression by being well groomed from head to toe.

Make sure your clothes are spotless and free of lint and wrinkles. If you have a long drive to your interview, wear casual clothes for the trip and change into your interviewing outfit when you arrive.

Go easy when applying perfume, cologne, aftershave or body lotion. In fact, your safest bet is not to wear any fragrance at all. If you've showered and used an antiperspirant, that should do it. An overpowering scent is a big turnoff in an interview, or in any business setting for that matter, and will detract from a good first impression. Remember the image you're trying to convey. You're not looking for a date, you're looking for a job offer!

Investing $10 on a good manicure is also a pretty good idea—and that doesn't apply to women only! Quite a few of the young men I work with spend their summers doing yard work and construction labor. For those candidates, a manicure is almost mandatory. Clean, trimmed nails are a must, even if your hands have been roughened through manual labor.

Women should trim nails to a reasonably short length, and make sure they're all the same length. Use only clear or see-through pink nail polish. Stay away from bold colors, acrylics, and bright red polish.

GOOD NEWS

Follow these simple hygiene rules: Your "first impression halo" will positively shine! I guarantee it!

They'll only detract from the conservative, professional look you're trying so hard to achieve.

Next comes hair—a pretty sensitive issue for many people. Some of you may not like to hear the advice I'm offering, but I must tell you that it is based on observation, general business policies of the companies I work with, and the feedback I've received from hundreds and hundreds of interviewers.

Men, keep your hair neatly trimmed, combed, and comparatively short. Ponytails are out of the question. As for beards and mustaches, you should know that companies with conservative dress codes, health-related industries, and manufacturing companies often frown on facial hair. In fact, beards and mustaches are prohibited in the manufacturing facilities of most food and chemical industries for reasons of safety and hygiene. If company policy doesn't allow facial hair and you walk into the interview with a beard or mustache, you run the risk of having one big strike against you.

If you insist upon keeping your facial hair, make sure it's clean, trimmed, and well groomed. My advice, however, is that you shave off that beard and mustache, and go clean-shaven throughout the interview process. Once you secure a firm job offer, you can begin to grow another beard or mustache, if company policy allows.

Most professional women keep their hair cut at shoulder length or shorter. A long, flowing mane of hair is fine for the heroine of a romance novel, but it's out of place in most companies. Long hair can be styled so that it's off your shoulders. Avoid the teased and heavily sprayed "fluff chick" look. Don't use gels or a lot of styling spritz (that goes for the guys too!). Your hair, like your clothing, should be very conservative.

Conservative is also the rule when it comes to makeup. Apply your makeup very sparingly. Use subtle colors of blush and lipstick. Save the bright, flamboyant lipsticks, the false eyelashes, and the rest of the goop for Halloween. Avoid bright eye shadows. In fact, you can skip the eye shadow all together. When you've applied your makeup properly, you'll look as though you're not wearing any at all!

Pardon me if I sound like your Mom, but my last tip for good interviewing hygiene is really important. Make sure you brush your teeth and rinse with a mouthwash before the interview! Nothing will spoil that first good impression quicker than a whiff of bad breath. To avoid that problem, quite a few of my clients carry a toothbrush or small bottle of mouthwash with them, particularly when they're scheduled for an all-day interview. Be prepared!

Finally, you've put your act together and you're ready for that all-important interview. You walk in the door. You look great. Now

WAKE-UP CALL

Don't, under any circumstances, chew gum or mints in your interviews.

what??? Should you begin by shaking hands with the interviewer? The answer is *yes*!

Believe it or not, your handshake can have a great deal of impact on your first impression. I've interviewed thousands of people over the years and am continually amazed by the number who don't take the initiative to shake my hand at all. I actually have to tell them a good handshake is good business etiquette!

A dynamic handshake is made up of five ingredients, all working together. If you're missing one of these ingredients, your handshake probably leaves room for improvement. Here are the five ingredients for a great handshake:

1. Make sure your handshake is firm and healthy. "Firm" means the hands interlock between the thumb and index finger, it doesn't mean a death grip. When your hands interlock, it's a solid handshake and there's no need to squeeze the other person's hand. A healthy handshake is accomplished by shaking the hand up and down once or twice. Don't extend a limp, lifeless hand, unless, of course, you want to be remembered as a dead mackerel.

2. Regardless of gender, shake the person's hand the same. A lot of young men shake my hand by grasping my fingers from the second knuckle down—as if they plan to kiss it and ask me on a date. Worse yet, they don't extend their hand at all. As I mentioned earlier, I'm surprised at the number who fall into the second category.

    When I questioned my candidates about their handshakes most of them told me that, because I'm a woman, they shook my hand differently, or used that as the reason for not having done so at all. Gender should make no difference. A woman who has risen to management got there because of her business savvy. She expects the same treatment as her male counterparts and if you don't deliver, it's a strike against you.

    And I'm not picking on just the guys! Young women are equally negligent when it comes to handshakes. In fact, not only do they do it incorrectly, they are more guilty than the men when it comes to not shaking hands at all!

    In the interview, you want to project the image of a business professional. So regardless of gender, yours or theirs, shake hands by the rules!

3. It's up to you to take the initiative! Today, it's not always the best-credentialed candidate who gets the offer; it's often the candidate who gives the most dynamic interview. When you take the initiative to extend your hand to the employer, you enhance your personal dynamics. You'll appear self-confident, mature, and assertive—exactly the kind of candidate that most employers look for in their potential hires.

4. Always introduce yourself! By all means, tell people who you are. Your introduction can be as simple as, "Good afternoon, I'm Richard Jones and I'm very pleased to meet you." Or, "Hello, I'm Richard Jones and I'm really looking forward to our interview today." Actually, the possibilities are endless. Say whatever you want to, just make sure you introduce yourself.

5. Always rise to your feet when shaking hands and making your introduction. For one thing, direct eye contact during the handshake has more impact and improves your personal dynamics. You want to look the interviewer in the eye, not the belt buckle. Body language is a powerful way to communicate. By standing up for the handshake, you put yourself on equal ground with the interviewer. If you remain seated, you concede that you're in a subservient or lower position. The employer is looking down on you and is in control.

DAMAGE CONTROL

Here's one last tip. Do you suffer from sweaty, clammy palms? Don't worry—there's a cure! Go to a bowling alley and buy a resin bag. Bowlers use them to keep their hands dry and to prevent the ball from slipping from their fingers. Rubbing the resin bag on your palms before the interview will keep your hands free of sweat.

The goal is to do whatever you can to put yourself on an equal footing with the interviewer. If your handshake and introduction are professional and dynamic, the employer will perceive you as more of an equal from the start.

Effective eye contact

Always look the interviewer directly in the eye when shaking hands and introducing yourself. Direct eye contact gives your introduction more positive impact. It conveys self-confidence, maturity, honesty, and a sense of self-esteem. In fact, eye contact is important not just for your introduction, but throughout the interview.

Poor eye contact during an interview telegraphs a lot of negative messages. If you fail to maintain eye contact, the employer may decide that you could be any one or more of the following: scared, disinterested, nervous, insecure, dishonest, or lacking in confidence or self-esteem.

By maintaining a "soft focus" throughout the interview, you'll eliminate the possibility of the employer drawing those negative conclusions about you. "Soft focus" means simply looking in the general direction of the person you're speaking to without looking them directly in the eye.

Breaking eye contact with the employer and looking away is okay if it's done briefly and infrequently.

Direct eye contact and soft focus are equally important in an interview. But you have to know *when* and *how* to stare the interviewer in the eye in order to be effective. Too much direct eye contact not only makes the other person uncomfortable, it also diminishes in impact if overused.

Reserve the focused stare for those times in the conversation when you want to emphasize a point or enhance your personal dynamics. When making your case on issues such as your willingness to relocate, look the interviewer in the eye. Your candid, open look will help to convince the employer that you're serious—that you mean what you say.

Body language

Your hands

Words aren't the only way to communicate. Quite a lot of people express themselves with their hands. If you do use your hands when you talk, continue to do so. People who use their hands in communication come across as more animated, more dynamic. As with good eye contact, using your hands will help you place emphasis on those points you want to drive home to the employer.

Don't go overboard, though. Pretend that there's a Plexiglas box around your chair, and keep your hand movements within those imaginary boundaries. Waving your hands around like a windmill can cause an unnecessary distraction. The employer's train of thought will be interrupted. Instead of listening to what you're saying, the employer will be watching what you're doing.

Unless you're the type of person who already expresses yourself with your hands, don't start now. If you're not comfortable using your hands in conversations, chances are that any attempt to use them in the interview will come across as contrived or unnatural.

Last but not least, don't hold anything in your hands while you're in an interview. That means your pen, resume, portfolio, lucky charm, or anything else. Eventually, you'll end up "playing" with it and creating a distraction or annoyance.

Your legs

Crossing your legs in an interview is generally unacceptable. We may be approaching the twenty-first century, but men are still men and women are still women. When an attractive young woman crosses her legs, she runs the risk of creating a distraction—not to mention the fact that crossing and uncrossing your legs in the interview increases the fidgeting factor. And you don't want to fidget in an interview.

Young men have a tendency to become too relaxed in their posture when they cross their legs. Slouching and poor posture don't convey a very businesslike image. Chances are, the interviewer will think you're disrespectful and that your slouching reflects your attitude about work and life in general.

My advice to both men and women is that, if you feel compelled to cross your legs, cross them at the ankle and keep your feet under the chair. You won't generate any negative impressions that way.

Posture

Don't underestimate the importance of your posture in an interview. How you stand and sit tells the interviewer a great deal about you. You have to find the middle ground.

When you stand, you don't want to look like a wooden soldier—but do keep your spine straight, your shoulders back, and your head up. When you sit down, plant yourself firmly on the chair. You can start the interview by "sitting at attention," but a few minutes into the conversation, you should adopt a more relaxed position. You *do* have to relax a little bit, but not so much that you slouch or are stoop-shouldered. Just don't get too relaxed. On the other hand, maintaining a stiff, rigid posture throughout the interview isn't good either. I frequently get feedback from recruiters who tell me that the candidate seemed tense, sat on the edge of the chair, and never relaxed.

When chemistry comes into play

There's no doubt that chemistry can be a factor in formulating a first impression. Unlike your personal appearance, handshake, eye contact, and body language, though, you have no control over chemistry—good or bad.

There are times when you will naturally "click" with an employer. The chemistry is good and you seem to make a connection with the interviewer.

On the other hand, it's also likely you'll run into an interview where the chemistry is bad. You'll feel as though the interviewer would rather be anywhere else on earth than talking with you, and may appear distracted, disinterested, or even impatient.

TRAPS TO AVOID

When bad chemistry takes place, you'll almost always detect it within the first five minutes of the interview. *The best advice I can offer when you sense bad chemistry is don't dwell on it.*

Typically, first-time job seekers will take the employer's attitude personally. It's only natural to do so. Five minutes into the interview, you're sitting there wondering what you've done wrong. "Is it my resume?" "My lack of experience?" "My credentials?" "What have I said that was so bad?"

Fifteen minutes into the interview, the thoughts turn to an attitude of defeat. "What's the use?" "I can't wait till this is over." "What a waste of time." You want to throw in the towel, and you end up using so much mental energy wondering what's wrong or wishing it would end that you don't focus on asking the next best question or giving the next best answer.

If you've done everything necessary to create a good first impression, chances are the employer's attitude has nothing to do with you or your credentials. Don't accept any of the blame for the employer's bad attitude. Shift the blame back to the employer.

Remember, an interview is an interruption of the daily routine of a department manager. There are a lot of other things on a manager's mind besides your interview, including budgets, production quotas, employee problems, and so on. Or the problem could be something else. Maybe the interviewer had a fight with a spouse before getting to the office or had to change a flat tire in the rain on the way to work.

Maintain your focus, give the best possible answers, ask relevant questions, and I guarantee you'll distinguish yourself from those who interview before and after you. At the end of the day, the employer will remember *you* as a more focused, mature candidate.

DAMAGE CONTROL

No matter how discouraged you may feel, don't be like the typical first-time job seeker who gives up midinterview. Focus your mental energy on interviewing well instead of wondering what you might have done wrong, and you'll not only succeed in the interview, you'll excel.

13

Interview Questions
How to Answer 50 of the Toughest

Shannon and I were on the last leg of our counseling sessions before she was about to go on the first interview I'd arranged for her. Like all of my clients, Shannon had to go through an Interview Prep before she met the employers face-to-face.

During our session, I asked Shannon to tell me the toughest interviewing question she'd ever been asked in an interview. She told me she had been in a couple of situations where the employer started the interview with, "So, tell me a little about yourself."

Suddenly, her throat was dry. She felt tongue-tied. She didn't know where to begin or exactly what to say. She found the question both challenging and intimidating. In fact, that particular question is one that strikes a fearful chord in most first-time job seekers, and for the same reasons Shannon gave.

Now that she had been through her personal inventory and had researched her market and job descriptions, Shannon's confidence was high. She told me that the question didn't seem nearly as intimidating as it was in the interviews she'd had before becoming my client. Instead of seeing it as a difficult question, Shannon began to realize that the question offered her a great opportunity: the opportunity to sell herself!

You'll feel the same way after you've read through the first twelve chapters of this book. Once you've taken your personal inventory, researched the job descriptions, and brushed up on your communication skills, your attitude about those "tough" questions will change just as dramatically as Shannon's did. In fact, as you read through the list of questions, you'll discover that most of them are simply giving you an opportunity to sell yourself to the employer.

Since I'm a big believer in being totally prepared for an interview, I decided years ago to put together a list of questions frequently asked in interviews. If I had asked the employers to supply me with the questions they intended to put to my clients in an interview, they probably would have responded with a resounding *no*. So, instead, I put the list together with the help of my candidates.

My clients were instructed to call me after every interview so that I could get some feedback on how things went. I asked each of them to make an effort to remember four or five of the most challenging questions the employer asked them. In a very short period of time, and with their help, I was able to compile a list of 50 questions most commonly asked in interviews.

Eventually, I decided to incorporate the list into my counseling sessions as a "homework" assignment. I ask each candidate to take the questions home and write their answers on a sheet of paper. When they return the next day, we go over the questions together and discuss the impact their answers might have on their interviews.

Although I'm unable to give you the kind of personalized service my clients get, I can, at the very least, share the list of questions with you and make a couple of suggestions. First, you can prepare yourself by writing down your answers to the questions as my clients are told to do. Then ask a friend, neighbor, or relative who works in a professional capacity to go over your answers with you and evaluate your responses. Don't solicit the help of a professor. Now, don't misunderstand—I have nothing against professors. It's just that they usually have very little real-world experience and might even offer advice that could do you more harm than good.

Next, have a friend or family member take you through a mock interview. Get their feedback and, if warranted, make the necessary adjustments to improve your interviewing style.

Most people fear the unknown. So it's okay if your knees shake a little before you go into an interview. But believe me, if you walk into an interview armed with the questions you know they'll be asking you, there's nothing to fear. That's especially true if you've already evaluated your strengths and are comfortable talking about them. The bottom line is that you'll be able to relax more in the interview and you'll impress the employer as a confident, self-assured candidate—head and shoulders above your competition.

TRAPS TO AVOID

The worst thing that can happen from having access to this list is that you'll turn yourself into an interviewing robot. *Don't practice too much!* If you labor too long and hard over these questions, you run the risk of becoming too pat in your answers and you'll come across in the interview as unnatural and rehearsed.

Because every one of you has an individual background, education, and career track, each of you will respond differently to these questions. For that reason, it's impossible for me to give you the "right" answers. But, in order to help you formulate *your own* best answers, I've made suggestions and comments or have given examples following each question.

Now, here's one last and very important recommendation.

First interview questions

1. What are your short-range goals, and how do you plan to achieve them?

Most graduates respond to this question by saying their short-term goal is to get their career started—in other words, to get a job. Since most graduates respond this way, any other answer will help you stand out from the competition. In fact, getting your career started would be the *immediate* goal. *Short-range* usually means a period of three to five years.

Your answer to this question should focus on your career goals and where you hope to be five years into the future. How do you plan to achieve that? The way all goals are achieved ... through hard work, self-motivation, and perseverance.

2. What personal goals have you set for yourself, and what do you hope to achieve over the next five to ten years?

Most graduates fail to see or hear the word "personal" and invariably respond to this question by stating a career goal. Another mistake a lot of candidates make is to indicate a desire to start and run their own businesses someday. If, indeed, that's your goal, keep it to yourself during an interview! The employer wants a rooted, stable, and responsible employee—someone who will be loyal to the company, not someone who is dreaming about being self-employed.

A good answer to this question might be related to marriage, buying a home, and having a family. Or, it could be something like training for and winning the Boston Marathon or the Iron Man Competition. It could even be that you'd like to write the great American novel.

Women should be careful when answering this question. You may say you'd like to start a family, but you have to convey it to the employer properly. A lot of women put their careers on hold or quit altogether when their first child comes along. For that reason, many employers are reluctant to invest in someone who's going to commit to the company for only a short period of time. It's okay to say you'd like to have children, but let the employer know that your career is what's most important to you. Furthermore, be sure to state how confident you feel about the challenge of handling both career and motherhood when the time arrives.

3. What are some of the most important rewards you expect from your career?

A good many people respond to this question by saying they expect to earn a lot of money. Be warned! If you say "money" or "material rewards," you'll have a strike against you unless you state your case properly.

When interviewing for sales, being motivated by money is a good quality to have. But you can't just answer by saying you expect to make a lot of money. You can say something like, "I hope to earn a lot of money in a sales career and, in the process, derive satisfaction from achieving my goals and being recognized by my employer for the contribution I've made to the company."

Other good responses might deal with personal or professional growth, the respect of one's peers, achievement of goals, contribution to the growth of the organization, etc.

4. What's more important to you, how much you earn or the type of job you have?

To me, the answer is obvious, but I'd say 10 percent of my clients felt how much they earned was more important than what they did. What you're being paid does make a difference, but it's not all that matters. You can earn big bucks, but if you hate your job, believe me, you'll be miserable.

What matters most is what you do, whether or not you do it well, and whether or not you're happy with what you're doing. If you're well suited to the job description, the likelihood is that you'll not only do it well, but you'll be happy with what you're doing. Eventually, you'll meet your earnings potential and on the way you will have experienced satisfaction in your profession.

5. What made you decide on this particular career?

How you answer this question depends upon the job title and responsibilities. Your answer should show the employer how your potential strengths tie into the job description.

A good answer would be, "My research tells me that people succeed in this career if they are strong communicators, good problem solvers, can work well under pressure, and have the ability to set and achieve goals. I feel these are some of my greatest strengths and, therefore, I would do well in this type of position."

6. Tell me what you feel your greatest strengths are. What about your greatest weaknesses?

Certain questions pop up in almost every interview—and this is one of them. To give a proper response, select three or four of the strengths from your personal inventory that match the job description and tell the employer what they are and how they fit in.

As for weaknesses, you should always be prepared with two examples even though most employers are satisfied with just one. Always focus on a weakness that can be turned around into a potential strength. If you need help with this one, refer to the section in Chapter 3 that deals with identifying weaknesses.

7. What motivates you to put forth the greatest effort?

The possibilities for advancement, the personal gratification you'd have as a result of meeting your goals, the respect of your peers, or the recognition from an employer for a job well done—all of these are good answers that will reflect positively on you.

8. How would you describe yourself?

Unless you've already been asked what your strengths are, you'll want to make sure you hit on a couple that fit the job description. If you have been asked what your strengths are, you don't want to repeat yourself if you can help it.

This question is an excellent opportunity to tell the employer a little about yourself on a more personal level. To describe yourself, you might use words like energetic, optimistic, fun-loving, easy to get along with, enthusiastic, possessing a good sense of humor, able to handle criticism well, self-confident, and so on. Although they may have nothing to do with the job description, all of these are considered positive qualities. They have a lot to do with telegraphing what kind of person you are.

This question also permits you to talk about your character traits like generosity, trustworthiness, and dependability. Personally, though, I feel your time is better spent selling other qualities about yourself. Remember, your character is assumed to be good unless your words or actions prove otherwise. So why waste precious selling time on qualities that have already been naturally accepted by the employer as being good? (See Chapter 4 for more information on character traits.)

9. How do you think a family member or friend who knows you well would describe you?

Base your answer on the same reasoning used in the previous question.

10. Tell me how college has prepared you for a business career.

Don't talk about your finance class, your last economics term paper, or your marketing research project. Talk about the leadership or management skills you learned through participation in clubs, organizations, or athletics. Get into the time management abilities and work ethic you developed as a result of juggling a job, extracurriculars, and a full course load. Get the idea?

11. What do you think it takes to be successful in a company like ours?

To answer this question you'll need to know the job description and something about the management style and personality of the company. It's a perfect example of why it's *so important* to research each company before the interview. When you know what kind of management style the company has, and the type of person who's typically recruited for the position, you'll know what qualities about yourself to focus on in your answer.

12. How do you determine or evaluate your own success?

Every one of you will have a different answer to this question. Perhaps you measure your success by how quickly you learn new skills in comparison to others. Maybe you measure it by setting personal or professional goals, and then working hard to achieve them. Or, perhaps you evaluate your level of success based on the fact that your peers seek you out for advice or consult with you when confronted with a problem. Just don't say you measure success by how much money you make. It might very well be true, but it's not the best answer.

13. What kind of contribution can you make to this company?

Once again, the employer wants to know how you think your assets and abilities will tie into the job description and the company's management style.

14. What qualities do you feel are necessary to be a successful manager?

There are actually quite a few. And, of course, your response should focus on two or three qualities that are, not coincidentally, potential strengths of yours.

You can select from a long list of qualities including time management, multitask orientation, the ability to motivate others, organizational and planning skills, the ability to make decisions, empathy, problem solving, strong communication skills, leadership, and more.

15. What two or three accomplishments in your life have given you the most satisfaction and why?

Almost all recent graduates include graduating from college as one of their greatest accomplishments. Since you don't want to give the same response as everyone else, give this question a little extra thought and try to recall an accomplishment that sets you apart from your competition. It doesn't have to be related to a job. Your answer can be of a personal nature, or related to sports, health and fitness, or other activities. Maybe you reached your goal of jogging ten miles, taught someone how to read, overcame a handicap, served as a pin-striper in your local hospital, scored a winning touchdown, won first prize in a music competition, or organized a soup kitchen. Whatever it is, now's the time to talk about it.

16. Why did you choose the college you attended?

There can be lots of different answers to this question, but the only one you shouldn't give relates to geographic convenience. Fortune 500 companies want candidates who are willing to relocate. If you chose your college because it was close to home and you wouldn't have to move, chances are employers will think you're blowing smoke when you tell them you're now willing to relocate for your career. It hurts your credibility.

17. What prompted you to choose your college major?

This question seems innocent enough, but it can be potentially harmful in an interview. It's a question that frequently puts graduates on the defensive.

If you changed your major more than two or three times, if it's a nonbusiness major, or if it's one that is preparing you for an advanced degree (e.g., pre-law, medicine, biology, chemistry, etc.), you're going to have some explaining to do. Whatever your answer is, just remember this: Don't make excuses—give explanations.

18. Do you have plans for continued education or an advanced degree?

This could be a little tricky. If you put too much emphasis on your plans for an advanced degree, the employer might think you're using them as a stepping-stone or vehicle for your continued studies. On the other hand, a majority of major corporations encourage an advanced degree and want candidates who are willing to make that type of investment in themselves.

I'd suggest you come up with an answer something like this: "Eventually, yes. But my immediate goal is to get my foot in the door of a major corporation, work hard, invest several years, and develop some career focus. That way, when I pursue my master's degree, I'll have a better idea as to what my concentration should be."

19. Which of your college subjects did you like the most and why?

The answer doesn't necessarily have to be the subject in which you got the best grades. Your favorite subject might have been the one where you were most academically challenged. Or perhaps it was a subject taught by a professor who motivated you in order to help develop your interest. Maybe the class gave you a chance to improve some of your skills like time management, leadership, public speaking, or problem solving. Think about it and come up with an answer that shows some depth and maturity.

20. Which of your college subjects did you like the least and why?

The trick here is to avoid being negative. Don't say, "I hated calculus," or whatever. Even if you didn't like a class, try to convey that you learned something, or grew in some way, as a result of having taken the course. And again, don't make excuses or blame your professor for your dissatisfaction.

21. Do you think your grade point average is an indication of your academic ability?

Well, was it? If it's less than a 3.0 and you worked over 25 hours a week, I'd say it's not. If you had a 3.5 GPA and didn't have a job, then I'd say it probably is a good indicator. Only you know for sure.

This is not the time to tell the employer any of your professor horror stories! You know, stories about how the professor was unfair and failed you on a test because you showed up late. Then you find out the test counted for two-thirds of your grade, which screwed up your overall GPA. So, if it hadn't been for him and that grade, your GPA would have been much better!

You'll be saying a lot of negative things about yourself with an answer like that. Yet surprisingly, one of the most common responses I get to this question is some type of professor horror story about being failed in a class or being graded unfairly.

22. What are some of the things you've learned from participating in extracurricular activities?

This is where you talk about team playing, leadership skills, getting along well with people, and time management. It's just one more opportunity to sell your potential.

23. Which of your part-time jobs have you been most interested in and why?

Obviously, this answer will be different for everyone. The trick is to draw on the experience that was most educational or rewarding, or one that led to your personal growth and maturity in some way.

24. If you could write your own job description, what would it be?

Create an imaginary job description that gives you an opportunity to sell your strengths, or potential strengths, to the employer. Think of four or five skills you possess that you'd like to develop and perform on a daily basis.

Design the job description so it's not too far removed from the one for which you're interviewing. This is just one more good reason why it's essential to research the position before the interview.

25. Why do you want to come to work for this company?

Here's another one of those questions that gives you a chance to let the employer know you did your homework. In fact, you should always know at least ten facts about any company you interview with. Research things like when they were founded, what their annual sales or profits are, what the management style is, who their competitors are, how big they are, where their corporate headquarters are, etc. Then, when you're asked this kind of question, you'll have ten rounds of ammunition with which to fire back an answer to the employer.

26. What do you know about our company?

This is a variation on the previous question. Same principle, same type of answer.

27. What kind of criteria are you using to evaluate the company you hope to go to work for?

Be careful with this one. Don't start out by talking about benefits, salary, and tuition refund programs. They may very well be issues with you, but you're better off by focusing your answer on the company's size, stability, positioning in the marketplace, length of time in business, quality of training, management style, opportunities for growth, and so on.

28. What two or three things are most important to you in the type of career opportunity you want?

Again, avoid discussing benefits and what the company can do for you. This question isn't all that different from the preceding question, so you'll want to provide a similar answer.

29. Do you have a geographical preference and, if so, why?

First of all, don't limit yourself geographically. If you're asked this question, give a broad geographic boundary such as the East Coast, the Northeastern United States, the Southwest. Better yet, indicate that you're 100 percent open to relocation. Let the employer know that the quality of the opportunity is much more important to you than where it might be located.

If you do have geographic limitations, you'd better be prepared to give the employer a reason why. If your reason is that you'd miss your family or you can't afford to move, I suggest you rethink your answer. In point of fact, most recent college graduates can't afford *not* to move in order to get their career off the ground! And, as far as family goes, I made my case very clear in Chapter 5. If you are close to your family, you will remain so, whether you're 5 miles away or 500 miles away.

30. Would it bother you to relocate, either to get your career started or to take a promotion three years down the line?

There's only one correct answer to this question if you want a career, and the answer is "no!" If you are asked this question and you respond with a "yes," I guarantee you won't be asked back for a second interview. If the employer makes a point of bringing up relocation in the interview, it is usually because the position will eventually require you to move.

31. Are you willing to travel?

There are only two answers to this question, yes and no. There are no "maybes."

First of all, if you did your homework before the interview, you should know whether or not a job description includes travel. Saying that you don't want to travel or putting limitations on where, how much, or how far you'll travel probably won't get you the job. Furthermore, if you realize the job description includes travel and you're opposed to it, why bother going on the interview at all? In my opinion the only correct answer to this question is "yes"!

32. Tell me about a major problem you've encountered and explain how you dealt with it.

When employers ask this question, they're looking for evidence of maturity and problem-solving ability. Try to focus on a problem of a personal or professional nature and avoid discussing your education, e.g., getting a term paper completed by the deadline.

33. Tell me something you've learned as the result of having made a mistake.

Even though we've all made mistakes, and plenty of them by the time we're in our early twenties, it's amazing how many people take too long to answer this question or don't come up with an answer at all.

Although this isn't the type of question you'll get in every interview, it's a good question for an employer to ask. Regardless of the mistake you might have made, your attitude and answer will tell the employer a great deal about your character, perceptivity, and level of maturity.

34. Is there anything you're afraid of?

Caution! This is a trick question and there's only one wrong answer. Everyone is afraid of something, so anyone who answers "no" to this question is a liar. You can say you're afraid of the dark, spiders, snakes, marriage (usually gets a laugh), or even failure, but by all means, tell them you're afraid of something.

35. When was the last time you got upset with someone? Tell me how you handled it.

This is an excellent interviewing question. It gives the employer a chance to zero in on the candidates with management potential. How you respond will give the employer an idea of how well you get along with others. Are you empathetic? Are your problem-solving and decision-making skills pretty good? Do you have the potential to manage the activities of others?

36. Which boss did you do your best work for? Tell me why.

Pick whichever boss you want. What the employers are looking for is evidence of growth. What did you learn? They want to hear things like, "I liked Mr. Jones best because, after showing me how to do something once, he left me on my own and trusted me to get the job done. He didn't check on me all the time and I liked that." Or, "I really liked Ms. Atwater because she allowed me to work outside of my job description. When my work was done, she gave me the opportunity to work on special projects." Or, "I liked Tom Watts the best. He was a tough manager, but I learned a lot from him about dealing with people in stressful situations and getting deadlines met."

Select an employer who taught you something. Perhaps you learned some of the fundamentals of management, or how to deal with people more effectively. Focus on a strength or two you've developed as a result of having worked for this person.

37. With [name of one of your former employers], did you ever decide to go against company policy to get something done? If so, what was the situation?

Another tricky question! You *never* go against company policy. You might try to work to change policy, but you never, ever break it.

38. With [name of specific company], did you ever have to do anything out of your ordinary job duties? Tell me what the situation was, and whether or not it upset you?

This is a good question that employers like to ask. Your answer helps them gauge your attitude regarding work ethic. In an interview, your attitude is under constant scrutiny and is one of the barometers the employer uses to measure you against other candidates. Projecting an "It's not my job" attitude, or telling the employer you did the work although it should have been someone else's responsibility, will put you out of the running. You'll never see a second interview.

Ask yourself if you're the kind of person who goes the extra mile, stays late if necessary, or seeks out additional work when your initial job assignment is complete. If that describes you, you shouldn't have any problem coming up with a good example for the employer.

39. Which person or event in your life has had the biggest influence on you?

Your answer to this question will help to set you apart from the competition. Most recent grads are so focused on selling their education in an interview that they overlook other segments of their lives. So don't limit yourself by focusing on a professor or the fact that you got a degree. This is the kind of question that should prompt you to look a little more closely at yourself. Think beyond the obvious and you'll be amazed at what you come up with.

40. Have you ever used input from your subordinates while serving as a manager or supervisor? If yes, explain.

Employers like to hear a strong affirmative in response to this question. Answer with, "When I'm the boss, my word is final!" and you show a dictatorial attitude that indicates poor management potential to employers. So don't come across sounding like Genghis Khan!

A really good manager utilizes input from subordinates. As a team leader, a manager is responsible for orchestrating a group effort in order to do the most efficient, effective job. When a manager is approached by a member of the team with a suggestion on making the system more efficient and effective, wouldn't it make sense to listen? Being a manager doesn't necessarily mean having all the answers all the time.

41. What did you like best about your job with [name of past employer]? What did you like least about it?

You may be tempted to give negative responses to these questions. *Don't.* The employer might ask this question about your job waiting on tables, instead of asking it about the internship you held. And you might be thinking you didn't like *anything* about your job waiting on tables. Just don't say it.

Focus on the positive. Even when you point out what you liked least, always talk about what you might have learned or how you might have grown from the experience. How you answer this kind of question tells the employer a lot about your attitude.

42. What do you do in your spare time?

Just tell them what you do, but make sure it's something with some substance and that it's apolitical. In other words, the activity could be writing, music, a physical fitness program, raising lop-eared rabbits, or volunteering at the local homeless shelter. But, even if it's true, don't say that your pastime is going to right-to-life meetings, being active in the NRA, or organizing marches for NOW or a gay rights group. Stirring up controversy is *not* one of your interviewing objectives.

Second and third interview questions

You're usually asked the following types of questions in second and third interviews. Your answers provide employers with an excellent barometer of your maturity and problem-solving and decision-making skills, as well as insight into your potential for management.

43. Have you ever missed a deadline? What were the consequences and how did you deal with them?

44. When was the last time you had to make a decision quickly? What was the outcome?

160

45. Tell me about a decision you've made that required a lot of thought. What was the result?

46. When was the last time you had to delay making a decision?

47. Tell me about a stressful situation you've been in and how you handled it.

48. Have you ever made an impact on a group of people?

49. Tell me about a time when you were disappointed in your performance.

50. Have you ever made a sacrifice in order to achieve a goal? If so, explain.

These last eight questions deal with situations and the answers require more thought, leaving most candidates dumbfounded and fumbling for something to say. Typically, their responses end up having to do with college classes, research projects, tests, or term papers. Don't fall into that trap. These are important questions, and the answers you give can have a great deal of impact. They'll help the employer to distinguish you from the people who interview before and after you.

Knowing these questions in advance of your interview gives you ample opportunity to take all the time you need to recall relevant situations that you can give as examples. Think about your answers now, and you'll eliminate the uncomfortable pause that usually results when the employer asks the question.

These fifty questions are by no means a complete and total representation of what you'll encounter in your interviews. As I mentioned earlier, my clients had a hand in this, and the questions I chose to include were those they felt were the most difficult.

You'll also be faced with questions regarding specific skills, aptitudes, and job-related tasks associated with the position. Since you've conducted enough research in advance to determine whether or not you're equipped for the responsibilities of the job, questions of that nature should be a piece of cake to answer.

GOOD NEWS

It's natural to feel a little overwhelmed by the prospect of facing all of these questions in an interview. But for heaven's sakes, *don't panic*! This list represents the kinds of questions asked of hundreds of candidates by different employers and recruiters in a variety of industries. The chances of your being asked all of them in any given interview are just about zilch.

Finally, I want you to remember that there really aren't any right or wrong answers to most of these questions, but there are definitely *good* and *bad* answers.

When you go through this exercise, take enough time to reflect on all of the positions you've held from your first job to your last. Take a good, hard look at your college career as well. Then focus on those experiences that would help you to telegraph some depth and substance when giving your answers. A well-thought-out answer to any one of these questions will go a long way in setting you apart from your competition.

14

Job Descriptions
Exactly What Do You Want to Do?

He wanted to make a career move, but didn't know what to do.

Dan had a BA degree with a major in Criminal Justice and a minor in Sociology. Both of his parents were government employees and they had a lot of influence on his choice of education and career path. Through his mother's connections, Dan was able to secure interviews and land a job as a social worker shortly after graduating from college.

When Dan came to me, he had been in the position for about a year and a half and was very unhappy with his career choice. His job description required him to conduct intake interviews, process paperwork, and make follow-up calls relating to cases of abused or neglected children and battered spouses. He found the job depressing and extremely frustrating. Daily contact with the victims of domestic violence, as well as dealing with the bureaucracy within his department, was making him miserable. On top of that, his compensation was much lower than that of some of his friends who were working in the private sector.

Dan knew he wanted to make a career move but didn't know what he was equipped to do in corporate America. What kind of job could he get with a liberal arts education and a government-related work history? Dan had no idea.

We worked on his inventory together and after learning more about him, I suggested he pursue a career in the insurance industry. Dan's response to the suggestion was, "Insurance? No way. You probably have to start out as an agent and I don't want to sell insurance policies."

In less than a minute, Dan discounted an entire industry and a variety of career opportunities because of a preconceived notion and a total lack of information. He didn't know what he didn't know!

I carefully explained to him that there were many opportunities available in the property, casualty, and health insurance industries that had nothing to do with sales. In fact, I pointed out, Dan's education, strengths, and skills were particularly well suited to a position in claims adjusting.

I gave Dan lots of background information regarding the industry, the different job descriptions, and how they interface with one another, and put him in touch with two of my previous clients who were currently working as adjusters.

In the process of doing his research, Dan's interest level in the industry, especially in the position of claims adjuster, increased dramati-

cally. He interviewed with three different companies for the same type of position and ended up getting offers from two of them. Not only did the information he gathered help Dan decide which career path to follow, it made him a better interviewee.

First-time job seekers are faced with a lot of unknowns. There's not only the problem of not knowing what they want to do for a living, but also the problem of not knowing just what kinds of jobs are available and, more importantly, what the jobs entail. Like Dan, you'll find that taking the time to research job descriptions and industries can have a significant impact on your success in landing not just any career, but the *right* career.

Making a good match not only increases your odds of success but helps minimize job-jumping early in your career. Also, like Dan, the insight you gain regarding the position and the industry will help you conduct a better interview. Your self-confidence will improve dramatically, and you'll be able to sell yourself more effectively to prospective employers.

I'll be covering a broad range of industries and opportunities in this chapter. Some offer formal training programs, and others offer either on-the-job training or no training at all.

My recruiting experience has been primarily in industries offering structured training in a business or manufacturing environment. These opportunities are available in the largest numbers and generally offer better salaries and more stability.

I'm also including information about opportunities that I refer to as "the job away from the job you want." For example, being a collections trainee in a bank might not sound too glamorous, especially if you have a college degree. But banking is a competitive job market and almost always requires above-average credentials. If you're a business major with average or below-average grades, you could be unemployed for a long time if you hold out for the banking job of your dreams. Starting out as a collections trainee is an opportunity to get your foot in the door. It's the job away from the job you want, but with the proper attitude, work ethic, and motivation, you'll be where you want to be in a couple of years.

GOOD NEWS

This chapter isn't designed to be an encyclopedia of jobs and job descriptions. Its true purpose is to open your eyes to the importance and process of learning about job descriptions, as well as identifying the strengths and aptitudes possessed by people who are successful in particular fields. Armed with that information, you'll be able to key in more accurately on opportunities that require and match the strengths you've already developed. (See Chapter 3.)

In industries like advertising, journalism, broadcast communications, and the performing arts, starting out in the job away from the job you want is standard operating procedure. You can have a communications degree with a 4.0 GPA and a career goal of being an on-air personality, but I can almost guarantee you won't walk off the campus and into the studio. You'll probably spend several years in apprenticeship or support positions before you get your first crack at being on the air. In these industries, you usually have to pay some dues and learn the business from the inside out. Reaching your ultimate career goal is going to take a lot more time, sacrifice, and self-motivation than it is for someone seeking a career in underwriting, accounting, or computer programming.

If there's an opportunity or industry that interests you and it's not included in this book, check it out at the library. Most public libraries have a wide range of books and reference materials covering job descriptions in just about any industry imaginable.

Then, based on what you've read, select a few of the careers you find most interesting and head for the telephone.

Don't hesitate. Pick up the phone. Call the main switchboard of any company or organization and ask to speak with the person holding the job you're researching. Nine times out of ten you'll be connected when you explain the purpose of the call. For the best results you should contact at least one other person, preferably two. If you get just one person's opinion, you might catch them on a bad day and end up listening to a litany of negativity.

To help you make your choice, I'm including some of the specific strengths common to people who succeed in each field, examples of companies and/or industries providing opportunities in that area, as well as a few examples of what to expect once you land a position in that field.

Nailing down precise information on salaries is more difficult. That's because the size and location of the company will pretty much determine how much you'll be paid. For example, a position as an ac-

GOOD NEWS

The phone can be *the* most effective tool during this stage of your career planning. Being able to talk with someone who actually holds down the kind of job you're pursuing will give you much better insight and will be far more valuable than anything you'll find in a book. It's an excellent opportunity to hear all about the ups and downs of the job directly from someone who does it for a living, regardless of what "it" is. I don't know about you, but I'd rather have that information *before* I commit to a career, rather than find out about it after I've already started.

count manager for a Fortune 100 company could carry an annual salary in excess of $25,000, whereas the same or a similar position in a smaller organization might be stretching it to pay $15,000 a year.

The salaries I'm giving you are general figures with a very broad range. The low end is what you might expect in a smaller town and smaller company, while the high end represents what you might expect to earn in major metropolitan areas and larger corporations.

Remember that this exercise isn't about money. It's about discovering which careers will offer you the path of least resistance and the most job satisfaction, as well as a realistic evaluation of what kind of growth potential you might expect.

Account management

Account management is a job title that carries with it a wide variety of job descriptions from one company and industry to the next. I always tell my candidates not to get hung up on job titles, but instead to evaluate job functions. Account management is the example I use to drive my point home.

In large corporations, an account manager is responsible for just what the title implies—managing the account in order to keep the customer happy and coming back for more. In small to medium-sized companies, sales functions are tied into the account manager's job, thereby creating a whole new job description. I know some excellent account managers who couldn't sell potholders to their own mothers!

Sales, a position that requires a different set of skills and personality from account management, is covered later in the chapter. Make sure you have an understanding of what the company's definition of the job entails. If sales is an element, determine if you have what it takes to succeed in *both* areas before committing to an interview.

Successful account managers deal with multiple projects and tasks simultaneously and must be very well organized. Their communication skills, particularly verbal, should be well above average. They have to solve customers' problems and handle stressful situations with tact and expediency. These include such problems as missed service appointments, damaged goods, incorrectly routed shipments, invoicing problems, and so on. Basically, the account manager is the liaison between the client and all the other departments in the company. The ideal account manager is a team player, but doesn't hesitate to take the reins.

Where to look and what to expect

Positions in account management are readily available in virtually any industry and company, regardless of whether the company provides a service or manufactures a product.

To establish continuity with the client, employers look for candidates who are willing to spend at least two to three years in the position before seeking promotion or transfer.

An account manager is exposed to every department in the company on some level—materials handling, inventory control, customer service, billing, purchasing, distribution, transportation and logistics, product development, sales, etc. Interfacing with that many departments offers an excellent opportunity to learn and develop an area of specialization if you are so inclined.

Salaries can range from $15,000 to $25,000.

Accounting and audit

Accountants prepare and justify financial reports, while auditors examine and verify the accuracy of existing financial records. A successful accountant or auditor is an analytical thinker, with an aptitude for math and the ability to solve problems. Computer literacy and a basic knowledge of finance and accounting-related software packages are almost always requirements of the job.

The job description is pretty basic, but you should know that accounting and bookkeeping are two different careers, and that the stereotype of the nerdy introvert with a pencil protector in every pocket went out with the lava lamp.

In today's financial climate of corporate takeovers, mergers, and fluctuating stock markets, an accountant has become much more of an analyst, futurist, and money manager than the accountant of 30 years ago. For these reasons, two other key ingredients for success are above-average communication skills and the ability to negotiate effectively.

Where to look and what to expect

Naturally, the most abundant opportunities in accounting and audit are found in banking, payroll and accounting service companies, consumer lending, and accounting firms. But manufacturing and retail companies need auditors and accountants, too.

An accountant in an accounting firm serves in a line position, which means that the job function supports the reason the company is in business—it is at least partially a sales function. In manufacturing or service-related industries, an accountant or auditor is usually in a staff or support function. The line position usually offers more upward mobility and an opportunity to get into management more quickly.

As a junior accountant, you'll start out crunching numbers the first year or two. The job description might include a lot of data entry and support of management and it can, at times, get a little boring. Basically you'll be doing what you learned in the classroom, which is why your grades are such a big issue in this field. How well you did in college is usually indicative of how well you'll do on the job.

If your grades were lower than a 2.7 GPA, getting into the Big Six is a lofty goal. With lower grades, you might have to start your career in a position of lesser responsibility, such as benefits administration or accounts payable and receivable, and then work your way up.

Whether your goal is public or private accounting, there are opportunities to learn a number of specializations, e.g., tax accounting, government audit, cost accounting, budget analysis, and mergers and acquisitions. Generally, these jobs aren't available as entry-level positions, but require the investment of a few years of hard work and continued education.

Salaries can range from $14,000 to $28,000.

Advertising, marketing, and public relations

Dozens of positions are available within this grouping of industries. If you want to start a career in graphic design, account management, copy writing, art direction, market research, media buying, traffic management, typesetting, or production, this is where you get your start. I can't break down each job description but I can share with you, in general, the qualities demonstrated by most people who succeed in advertising, marketing, and public relations.

First of all, they're people who get along well with people, all kinds of people. They have to be team players. Everyone from the graphic artist to the production assistant to the writer to the account manager works very closely with one another, as well as with the client, to deliver concepts and campaigns that work.

Being able to handle stress well, being able to meet deadlines on or ahead of schedule, and being able to switch gears easily are all key ingredients as well. In my years in advertising I've seen many designers, art directors, writers, and production staff burn the midnight oil—not to mention the weekend oil—to rework an ad campaign in time to meet a publisher's insertion deadline. This is *not* an industry for clock watchers!

Much emphasis is placed on a positive personal image and above-average communication skills, both verbal and written. And, of course, the ability to be individually, yet collectively, creative is an essential ingredient.

Where to look and what to expect

Formal training programs in advertising, marketing, and public relations are few and far between. Those that do exist are usually available through a handful of the top national agencies and are generally located in major metropolitan areas like New York, Chicago, and Los Angeles.

But don't be discouraged. Before you pack your bags, look closer to home.

It's not easy to land a position as a graphic designer or a writer when all you have is an education and no portfolio. These are areas where an internship could be a key factor in getting your foot in the door.

If you really want a career in this industry, you'd better resign yourself to the fact that the easiest and fastest way to get started in advertising and PR is to start at the bottom and work your way up. I know this to be true from my own experience.

In my early career, I worked in the advertising department of the largest drug store chain in the country, and also spent a couple of years

GOOD NEWS

You don't have to move to the big city to land a career in this field. There are hundreds and hundreds of local and regional advertising and public relations agencies across the country in towns both large and small. In addition, major corporations who handle their advertising and public relations in-house offer the same opportunities you would find in an ad agency.

LOOKING AHEAD

Don't assume that a job as an account coordinator or traffic assistant is beneath you. Look at it as an opportunity to get your foot in the door, learn as much as you can, contribute whatever you can, and build a portfolio. Eventually, you'll land the job you really want.

in the creative department of the second largest business-to-business advertising agency in Ohio. We always had college interns on staff and when there was a hiring need, they almost always got first crack. The problem was, the jobs they got first crack at were not the jobs they really wanted. They were positions like secretaries (every secretary in the ad agency had a four-year degree!), assistants, and gofers. As I mentioned earlier, "the job away from the job you want" is more practice than theory in some industries.

The work environment is usually more relaxed and casual than it is in industries like banking or insurance, especially on the creative side. But it's also very high-energy and fast-paced. Last, but certainly not least, it's a pretty unstable environment as far as job security goes.

In this field, you are only as good as your last design, your last concept, or your last piece of copy or production. Billable hours are what drive agency employees. They should be able to bill the client for every job function they perform. The fewer billable hours you have, the more expendable you become.

When the account you're working on decides to pull its business and move to another agency or take the work in-house, heads roll. In regional and national agencies, there might be more than 50 staff members assigned to work as a team to support one client. That client might represent hundreds of thousands of dollars in revenue to the agency. When that account pulls its business, most of those 50 people will be out of a job. A few lucky ones might be reassigned. If you're really good at what you do, the client might ask its new agency to give you a job as part of the deal because they liked the work you did for them in previous campaigns. I've seen it happen many times.

Salaries can range from $14,000 to $23,000.

Banking

Most major banks offer a vast number of career opportunities including, but not limited to, commercial lending, internal audit, customer service, accounting, trust, retail bank management, personnel and administrative management, and computer programming. Defining each job within the realm of banking would fill a book, so I've provided general, overall descriptions for most of those positions in this chapter.

Specific job descriptions aside, some key attributes recruiters look for are leadership potential, good personal image, high verbal skills, active community involvement, and, because of the continually changing face of the industry and the economy, an interest in continued education.

Competition is very high for entry-level jobs in banking. To whittle down the large number of applicants, most recruiters place a great deal of emphasis on grades and internships during the initial resume screening. Surprisingly, the type of degree and major aren't usually a factor due to the wide variety of job descriptions available. Because of this, I've been able to place a lot of liberal arts majors in banking over the years.

Where to look and what to expect

Retail banks, commercial lending institutions, savings and loan companies, and credit unions all offer positions that are somewhat interchangeable in the financial arena.

Generally speaking, most banks provide training on a 12-month rotational basis. The employee "floats" through several different departments before being assigned to a permanent position. That's why it's important for you to familiarize yourself with a variety of job descriptions when interviewing for this type of career. But don't worry about that if you're a computer programmer or an accountant. In those cases, you're being interviewed for a specific position and there's usually no departmental rotation.

You can expect a very professional, structured, and conservative work environment. Although most people still think of banking as a 9-to-5 job, the banking industry has changed over the past few years. In retail banking in particular, you can expect to work a fluctuating schedule or shift. Within the bank's corporate headquarters, you'll find that many of the departments, such as customer service, computer programming, and credit information, function on a 24-hour-a-day basis.

Salaries can range from $18,000 to $28,000.

Computer programming

Programmer analysts are problem solvers. They're usually very analytical and have a very strong technical aptitude. You must also have an eye for detail, and a creative nature is a plus, especially if your goal is software development. Since computer-related products and programs are continually evolving and becoming more technically sophisticated with each passing day, the ability to learn quickly and easily is a valuable asset.

Being able to work well independently is a key factor but, as more and more companies become computer integrated, communication skills and being a team player are increasingly necessary to achieve success. Those two qualities also open more windows of opportunity for advancement into other programming-related positions such as computer consulting, sales, marketing, installation, systems security, software and hardware development, and engineering.

All of these positions are generally difficult to land if you're fresh out of college. Getting in the door as a programmer analyst is probably the best way to get started, but be careful not to pigeonhole yourself in the first few years on the job. It can happen very easily if you don't stay current on the latest software packages and new languages. Before you know it, you've spent three years using the same software and languages, and you find yourself behind the times.

LOOKING AHEAD

Because the industry is advancing and changing so quickly, taking the initiative to continue your education will almost always guarantee swifter movement up the corporate ladder. If the employer doesn't sponsor ongoing training, it's a good idea to make an investment in yourself and attend seminars on your own time and at your own expense. It will definitely pay off.

Where to look and what to expect

Headquarters of major corporations, communications companies, service-oriented industries, information service companies, and manufacturers of high-tech products offer a wealth of opportunities for candidates pursuing this field.

As with accounting, your grades will usually count for a lot in the hiring decision. How well you do in the classroom can be directly related to how well you'll perform on the job. In addition, pre-employment testing is common in this industry, and the results will definitely determine whether or not you land the position.

The computer industry, including hardware and software development and applications, is one of the premier growth industries in this country. For that reason, anyone with solid technical skills and a high degree of motivation should be able to move up and on rather quickly.

Salaries can range from $16,000 to $30,000.

Customer service and collections

Earlier in this chapter I mentioned that a position in collections is a great means of launching a career if you've made a few mistakes in managing your college education, for example, taking six-plus years to graduate, or having a very low GPA, or no extracurriculars. Collections can be the job away from the job you want. The same holds true for customer service.

DAMAGE CONTROL

Both customer service and collections positions have helped many of my clients repair the damage done during the college years. The price they paid was to start in a position they were equipped to handle, but one that wasn't exactly what they wanted to do and didn't come with the paycheck they were hoping for. What it offered was the chance to get back on track.

The key to your success will be finding a larger corporation whose benefits package includes tuition reimbursement and a policy of promoting from within. If you work on getting your advanced degree during the evenings and weekends, and commit to earning the highest possible GPA, you'll be able to rise above your situation in just a couple of years.

Customer service and collections positions require basically the same attributes. Both deal with the public, and most of the workday is spent on the phone and in front of a computer terminal. Obviously, above-average communication skills are necessary, as well as the ability to deal with all types of people from all walks of life. You never know who's going to be on the other end of the phone. Problem-solving skills, patience, and empathy also come in handy. If you're interested in moving up in the company, you'll need a strong goal orientation, self-motivation, and an excellent work ethic.

The primary difference between the two jobs is the stress factor. Customer service deals with solving the customer's problems and answering their questions. Now and then you might run across a surly customer but, generally speaking, you're there to help them in some way. In collections you're dealing with customers under less than ideal circumstances. You're trying to get money from them and, many times, they don't have it to give. They may be upset, angry, or even insulting. Whenever you're tempted to lose your cool, just remember that this is the job away from the job you want.

Where to look and what to expect

Customer service opportunities are available in nearly every type of company in both service industries and manufacturing. The same is true for collections, although many companies hire an outside collection service to do the job for them.

Customer service training programs are usually six weeks or less in length and deal primarily with providing an education on the product or service the company provides. Collections training programs are about the same length but focus more on handling people, dealing with stress and confrontation, and learning negotiation skills.

Salaries can range from $15,000 to $21,000.

Engineering

Basically, engineers design, assemble, test, maintain, and improve upon products, machinery, processes, and systems. They can function in positions as diverse as analyst, consultant, manager, salesperson, designer, troubleshooter, scientist, or field service representative, to name just a few.

Engineering is extremely diverse and encompasses many areas of specialization. Biomedical, chemical, industrial, quality, manufacturing, plastics, electrical, metallurgical, materials, aerospace, mechanical, computer, and civil are just a sampling of the different disciplines.

If you can eat or drink it, touch it, drive it, fly it, build something with it, walk on it, use it for communication, or wash your clothes with it, you can be sure an engineer was involved in its development in some way, shape, or form.

In fact, engineering positions in both manufacturing and service arenas are currently my specialization as a recruiter. The field is so enormous, I could easily write another book with the information I've gathered thus far. So if engineering is your chosen career path, I strongly suggest that you do some serious investigation of the field beyond what is offered in this book.

In very general terms, engineers have to be analytical, creative, have a strong orientation toward math and computers, and have the ability to conceptualize. They need to have good management skills because, in most cases, they are managing either people or projects. Therefore, organizational skills, communication skills, and the ability to make sound decisions are essential attributes.

Where to look and what to expect

Engineers are in demand in all manufacturing companies, in consulting firms, and in most service industries. Even in the worst of economic times, an engineering education is highly marketable.

Because of the tough curriculum associated with an engineering degree, most employers consider anything over a 2.7 GPA to be above-average. Those of you who have a GPA in excess of 3.0 should have practically no problems landing interviews.

Most medium-sized and large companies offer formal training programs, but the smaller organizations usually train on-the-job under the tutelage of a senior engineer. Some smaller companies might even start you out as a shift supervisor or maintenance mechanic until you learn the ropes of their specific industry.

Ongoing education is extremely important in this field, and most corporations willingly provide the training. Engineering is becoming very high-tech, so it's essential to stay on top of newly developed systems and software packages.

Additionally, engineering offers a wide choice of career opportunities within a variety of engineering disciplines, ranging from aerospace to biomedical to metallurgy. The key to getting ahead is to find the segment that interests you, and then go for it. Getting advanced training will help you develop an area of expertise and will insure your future marketability. For example, within the field of electrical engineering, you might specialize in any one of the following fields: controls, power distribution, research and development, circuit design, facilities, field service, sales, or software engineering. Within the first three to five years of starting your career, you should have been around the block enough times to determine which area of specialization is of greatest interest to you.

Your working environment will depend entirely upon your area of expertise. A civil engineer spends a lot of time outside, in the field or in an office trailer. A sales engineer is on the road and visits a variety of manufacturing facilities. An R&D metallurgical engineer might work in a laboratory, and a software engineer might work in a plush office environment. Regardless of your engineering discipline, your choice of specialization puts you in ultimate control of the work environment you wind up in.

Salaries can range from $20,000 to $45,000.

Government

For any position imaginable in the private sector, you can usually find an equivalent job in the realm of government. So, instead of talking about a specific job description, let's talk about the opportunities in government in general.

First of all, most people pursuing a career in government begin preparing very early on in their college careers. Whether you're participating in the ROTC program, getting involved in campus politics, playing an active role in local political campaigns, or taking an internship with government sponsorship, planning ahead is the key to your success.

People who pursue opportunities in government often have an altruistic nature and a desire to serve. Many are innovators who want to bring about change for the betterment of society. Some are drawn to careers in government because of the power associated with a position of leadership, while others are drawn to this field because they believe it provides more job security and better benefits.

Where to look and what to expect

Government jobs are available at the local, county, state, and national levels. Regardless of what your career focus is, you won't receive a lot of formal training but will most likely learn on the job. Expect to pay some dues in government. Starting out as a Congressional aide or secretary, or serving on an election committee as a gofer or receptionist is more the rule than the exception.

WAKE-UP CALL

Before you launch yourself into this orbit, however, be sure that a career in government is what you really want. Once you commit to a career in government, the likelihood is that you'll remain there. Should you decide that you want a job on "the outside," you'll find that the transition from a government job to the private sector isn't always an easy one to make.

You can also expect a lower-than-normal wage and comparatively slow growth in a government position. Only the most motivated, aggressive, and hard-working candidates experience meteoric success in government positions. Most often, who you know is more valuable than what you know when it comes to moving up the ladder. It should come as no surprise, therefore, that networking is an indispensable tool in this trade, regardless of the type of position you're considering.

Salaries can range from $14,000 to $28,000.

Insurance

Property/casualty and health insurance companies provide some of the most comprehensive training programs available. Although there is a wide variety of job opportunities within this field, I've decided to focus on two positions in particular. Both of them are available in large numbers, pay very good salaries, and can accommodate candidates with any type of degree or major. They are claims adjusting and underwriting.

Claims adjusters are primarily problem solvers. When a policyholder experiences the loss of a car, a business, a home, or even a life, the claims adjuster analyzes the situation to arrive at a settlement. Since the client has just lost something or someone very important, the claims adjuster's ability to handle people in stressful situations with tact, empathy, and a sense of urgency is of paramount importance.

Claims adjusters work not only with policyholders, but also with attorneys, investigators, police, physicians, and members of the property/casualty team, which includes loss control engineers, operations management staff, and underwriters. Because the industry, in general, is extremely people-oriented as well as team-oriented, above-average communication skills and the ability to deal effectively with a wide variety of people are important attributes.

Adjusters conduct investigations, research loss information databases, and manage litigation. They have an eye for detail, are organized, and are multitask-oriented, sometimes managing dozens of claims at one time. They are decision makers, negotiators, and project and people managers.

If you're interested in banking and finance and you haven't checked into underwriting, you're missing a big chunk of your job market. Underwriting is a large industry that encompasses many areas of specialization—each of which offers plenty of opportunities. As an example, you could pursue an underwriting career specializing in bonds, ocean marine, commercial lines, personal lines, energy resource, applied technologies, or executive protection, to name just a few. The wide variety of specializations opens this career to just about any type of degree or major.

Basically, underwriting is financial and risk analysis. People and businesses get insurance because they want to cover a potential loss or are at risk of losing something, whether it's a building, a boat, financial holdings, a car, a life, or a crop of grapes.

The underwriter analyzes the risk involved and decides whether or not to provide coverage making the insurance company financially responsible should something go wrong. It's not strictly financial analysis, though. Depending upon the branch of underwriting you get into, you could be asked to analyze how a computer virus might affect a bank, how to provide security on a multimillion dollar lakeside vacation home, how a strike might affect a transportation company, or how a drought might affect a wheat farmer. As you might imagine, underwriting is a position that carries with it a great deal of responsibility.

Successful underwriters are very thorough and well organized. They have good investigative skills and an eagle-eye for detail. They're extremely analytical but have the ability to think creatively. They're decisive and can solve problems easily. Their people skills and communication skills are above average, and they work well in a team environment. Most often, they assume the role of captain, making leadership and management skills an important part of the job.

Insurance represents a very big slice of the service industry pie. There are hundreds of property/casualty and health insurance companies out there. Better yet, it's a decentralized industry. Every branch within any given insurance company has the ability to hire and train.

Much like banking, insurance is a very conservative industry so it's not surprising that a lot of emphasis is placed on having a positive personal image. It's also an industry that promotes ongoing education. An advanced degree will get you farther, faster in the insurance industry.

Most insurance companies offer extensive, very structured training. It's possible to spend up to two years in training for some of the positions, with a good deal of that time spent in a classroom environment. It's also an industry that is technically in tune with the times. Good computer skills and a basic knowledge of a sampling of financial software packages will improve your chances.

Opportunities for growth are excellent, and most of the companies employ a "promote from within" policy that insures greater job stability. Due to the decentralized nature of the industry, promotions usually mean being relocated within the corporate structure. Realistically, if you're motivated to move up the corporate ladder, you can expect to move two or three times in the first ten years of your career.

Salaries can range from $17,000 to $29,000.

Sales

The best salespeople come equipped with equal amounts of ego drive and empathy. They have above-average interpersonal and communication skills. They're able to work well independently and plan their time effectively. They work well under pressure and are able to handle rejection. And, of course, the most successful salespeople have a high degree of self-motivation and are extremely goal-oriented. The job description can vary from one company to the next depending on the product and market.

There are quite a few careers that aren't pure sales, but combine sales with some other function. For example, service technicians working for a manufacturer or consulting firm are responsible for maintaining systems and equipment. Often, they have engineering backgrounds. When they go into a company to repair or maintain equipment, they also attempt to upgrade the customer by selling new or additional products or services. About 80 percent of what they do is service and maintenance, the other 20 percent is sales.

WAKE-UP CALL

Be aware that some job descriptions may include the word "sales," but they're essentially something else.

In positions such as consumer product sales, the job description is primarily merchandising, marketing, and order taking. The bulk of the job amounts to negotiating shelf space for products, setting up displays, organizing and fronting products, and making sure the customer has been receiving shipments on time and in good condition. I knew someone who did this for a living—he referred to himself as a glorified stock boy with a company car.

Both examples reinforce the necessity for you to research job descriptions. Despite the sales element, I doubt that a hard-charging sales type would find much job satisfaction in either of these two positions.

Where to look and what to expect

Sales opportunities are available in both service and manufacturing industries. Virtually every company that provides a product or service needs a sales force. That's a lot of companies—and a lot of sales jobs. Even though sales positions are available in large numbers, my experience has shown that it's a risky career path for the recent college graduate. It carries with it the highest failure rate—and that's especially true if it is a commission-only job.

TRAPS TO AVOID

Here's my best advice to a first-time job seeker: Avoid any sales position that doesn't offer a base pay or salary. The pressure to learn the job and meet your quotas, coupled with the pressure of having to pay your bills, is usually enough to guarantee your ultimate failure in the position.

A reputable sales training program will either have you on a permanent salary plus commissions, or will offer you a salary for the first year or two until you've established your territory. At that point, your compensation package changes to commissions and bonuses only. That's an acceptable arrangement because your account base has been established and your earned commissions provide a steady income.

The type of education you have is usually irrelevant. Technical or pharmaceutical sales are the exception. If you're pursuing those two areas, a degree in engineering, biology, pre-med, or chemistry is usually required.

Base salaries can range from $0 to $23,000.

Television, radio, and the performing arts

I've lumped these three industries together because I think the jobs they offer have a lot in common. Careers in television, radio, and the performing arts generally fall into three basic categories: behind the scenes, production, and talent.

Behind the scenes jobs are support jobs. They include positions in areas such as sales, secretarial, traffic, marketing, administration, publicity, and fundraising.

People with marketing, business, and communications majors often start out in broadcast communications as secretaries or traffic assistants just to get their feet in the door. The ones who succeed are the ones who are willing to roll up their sleeves and do anything that's asked of them in order to get the show on the air. An "it's not my job" mentality doesn't fly.

Production jobs involve getting the show on the air or the curtain raised. Jobs like sound control, lighting technician, cameraman, writer, producer, costume designer, director, print producer, stage manager, and prop coordinator fall into this category.

Some production jobs are technical (sound engineer), some are creative (script writer), and some are managerial (director). The good news for first-time job seekers is that these jobs commonly require back-up assistants.

Last but not least, there's talent—the performers, the singers and dancers, the disc jockeys, the voice-over artists, the news anchor, the weather person, or the sports announcer.

Getting on stage or on the air as a performer takes long-term dedication to the goal. Most people who succeed have been involved in their craft for many years before completing their education and entering the job market. To land their dream job they need a great deal of motivation, an above-average goal orientation, and the ability to handle rejection—and usually lots of it!

that, she was perfectly suited to the job description and was likely to do very well in the position. What more could she want?

Crystal agreed with everything I pointed out to her. So when she finally opened up, I couldn't believe my ears. The problem, she said, was that the company had given a start date two weeks from the date of the offer. She told me she couldn't possibly pack, move, find an apartment, and buy furniture and drapes in only two weeks.

She went on to say that in three weeks she was going to serve as maid of honor in her best friend's wedding and the rehearsal was on a Friday. She was concerned that she wouldn't be able to have the day off from work in order to fulfill her commitment to her friend.

That's it. Those were her only two reasons for rejecting the offer.

Crystal's real problem was that she was suffering from cold feet. She was overwhelmed with details and had lost sight of the quality of the opportunity and the significance of her decision.

Getting your first job offer can generate a lot of conflicting emotions. Fear, excitement, uncertainty, happiness, relief, confidence, apprehension, and more. But don't let your emotions take you on a roller-coaster ride. This is the time to be objective, not subjective. You want to clear your mind and focus your thoughts so that you can weigh your options and ultimately make a decision that will serve your best interests, now and in the future.

There are many facets to any job offer, and you'll have to consider all the pros and cons before you make a final decision. In this chapter, I'll talk about the elements of the typical job offer and the impact they might have on your particular situation. I'll also give you some tips on what to expect once you accept the position and start to work.

Before I get into the details, I think it's very important that you understand what makes a job offer a job offer. Over the years I've had many clients who were under the impression they had received an offer but, in fact, they had not.

WAKE-UP CALL

If an employer asks you when you can start to work, it's not a bona fide job offer! An offer is considered valid only when you've been given a start date *and* a starting salary by the employer. No ifs, ands, or buts!

Starting salaries

Many young people graduating from college have unrealistic expectations regarding what their education is worth to an employer in the job market. Reality hits when they receive their first offer.

Starting salaries at the entry-level aren't always the greatest. A lot of companies don't like to start a trainee out at a higher salary because the individual is still unproven. Most graduates are hired on the basis of their potential and not their experience.

Typically, entry-level salaries range between $17,000 and $30,000, regardless of whether the candidate holds a bachelor's or a master's degree. Entry-level positions paying more than $30,000 to start are usually confined to specialized fields such as chemical engineering, software engineering, electrical engineering, and so on. What you should consider at this point is what the company is offering above and beyond the starting salary.

I encourage my clients to look a little further than the ends of their noses. Find out what the company's policy is on evaluating and promoting their trainees. Ask about the trainees who were hired 12 to 18 months ago. Where are they now? What are they doing? What you'll discover may surprise you.

Usually, a trainee's performance is very closely scrutinized during the first year or so. It's not uncommon for a company to give multiple salary increases during that period of time if the trainee lives up to or exceeds expectations. Just as it was in college, not everyone performs at the same level or progresses at the same rate and speed.

This is one of the primary reasons why entry-level salaries usually aren't negotiable. Typically, when an employer makes an offer to a potential trainee, it's etched in stone. After all, what do you have to negotiate with? You and the other candidates under consideration are all lined up in the same starting position. You haven't yet done anything to distinguish yourself from the others. The company has to invest in training all of you. None of you has related experience. You all have potential, but how much can't be determined until you've started to work. So why should they pay you any more than the next guy to start?

Getting your first job offer is a lot different from getting an offer once you have a few years of experience. Then you *do* have something to negotiate with. Perhaps your competition has no degree and ten

LOOKING AHEAD

Look at it this way. If a company is hiring a total of four trainees in the first quarter, you are worth no more or less than the other three, even if you have a master's degree. Until you've proven yourself, the employer has no reason to start you out at a salary higher than the others. Now, at the end of 12 months, if you've learned faster, shown more motivation, worked harder, and invested more of yourself than the other three people have, then I can guarantee your salary at that point will be higher than the other employees who started at the same time.

years' experience, or a master's degree and six years experience. Then there's you, with a bachelor's degree and a few years under your belt.

The difference is this: You've all proven yourselves to varying degrees in the field in which you're interviewing. When you start working, you start working! Once you have a few years' experience, there's no question regarding your ability to perform and the company doesn't need to invest in training you. Your skills are measurable and your compensation will be in line with what you're bringing to the table, so to speak. It's just not the same when you're a trainee.

I suggest you don't try to negotiate a salary offer when being hired as a trainee. Not only for all the above reasons, but also because the market is so competitive.

Check out the benefits.

Aside from individual growth and salary potential, you also need to consider the benefits package. Some companies might offer a little more to start, but have less-than-adequate benefits. Maybe they don't have a tuition refund program, or they pay only a portion of your health insurance premiums.

On the other hand, a company that offers less to start might pay all of your health care benefits, offer tuition refund, or have an employee stock incentive program. Maybe they're willing to pay your relocation expenses, or there's a company car involved after training.

Before making your decision, find out what you're dealing with above and beyond the starting salary. Many times, the perks and other incentives offered by a company will compensate for the fact that your starting salary is a few thousand dollars a year less than what you were expecting.

All of the salary and benefits information is usually shared in a callback interview. Although I've said it before, it's worth repeating: *Never* discuss salary and benefits in the first interview! When the subject of salary and benefits does come up, it should be introduced into the conversation by the employer!

Of course, when you're being seriously considered for employment, you have every right to ask any and all questions related to the benefits being offered. When the time is right, don't be shy about asking for the information. It's absolutely necessary for you to gather all the details in this area in order to make an informed decision.

Remember, too, you have to maintain a positive attitude when you hear what the employer has to say regarding salary and benefits— even if you're not thrilled with the news. A positive attitude includes not just what you say, but your facial expressions and body language as well. Keep any negative feelings to yourself, unless you want to jinx the deal and watch the offer go up in smoke. Hear what the employer has to say, and don't react prematurely.

When you finally receive an official offer, you usually don't have to deal with it on the spot. It's okay to ask for a day or two to consider your options. Use that time to gather more information. Talk to people. Do some more homework. And don't just evaluate the opportunity in terms of today, look at where it'll take you five years from now.

Going to work

Once you accept the offer, be prepared to go to work at the employer's convenience. In other words, if they tell you they want you to start in one week, you'd better not come up with a slew of reasons why you'll need more time.

If, like Crystal, you have a previous commitment that might interfere with your ability to start, don't just turn down the opportunity. Take the advice I gave Crystal. Talk to the employer about your scheduling conflict. Remember, employers are human, too! Explain your situation and try to work out something both you and the employer can live with.

I'm happy to say that, ultimately, Crystal accepted the position as Business Analyst. When she approached the employer with the fact that she was committed to a wedding that was scheduled months ago, the employer understood her situation. She made no demands or stipulations; she simply explained the problem and left the decision up to the employer.

In Crystal's case, the employer gave her the option of moving her start date to the following Monday, or starting on the original date and taking the Friday off. The employer also offered to pay her for the day and charge it against the week of vacation she had coming after her first six months on the job. She took the second option and used the opportunity to coordinate her move to Pennsylvania in two trips instead of one.

Crystal's reaction to her offer is really more typical than you might think. Quite a few college graduates "freak out" when they're finally faced with an offer. All of a sudden they're overwhelmed by circumstances and details. They worry about who's going to help them move, how they'll find a place to stay, what they're going to wear (at this point, most of my clients own only one suit), how they're going to get their hands on a deposit and first month's rent, and on and on.

My advice is: *Calm down and get organized.* These are merely details, and if you approach them logically and systematically, they can easily be resolved. Any change in a person's life, whether good or bad, creates stress. Now's as good a time as any to learn how to deal with it.

Some of my clients have received offers and have gone to work within three days of acceptance in a city 500 miles from their home. If you want it badly enough, there's always a solution to the problem, whether the problem is real or imagined.

Relocating and finding a place to live

After accepting an offer, my typical client usually considers relocation to be the most overwhelming problem. Since that's the case, I'd like to share a few pointers with you so you can make the transition a little easier.

Those of you who are moving to a major metropolitan area should check what resources are available for apartment rental assistance. There are some businesses out there that specialize in locating roommates. It's a little like a dating service. You interview, indicate what your needs are, and pay a nominal fee for the company to match you up with a roommate. Most of you have spent the last four years in college rooming with people who were total strangers to you in the beginning. Look at it as another year of dorm living, only better.

In addition, many corporations have bulletin boards where you can post a notice regarding your apartment search. It's not uncommon for a trainee to wind up sharing an apartment with another employee of the company, or living temporarily in someone's guest room. Until you get established, it's a great way to make the transition to a new city.

Check out the Chamber of Commerce in the city you're moving to. Ask for assistance in securing apartment guides and have them steer you to those sections of town where the rental rates are in line with the income you'll be receiving. Getting help from the Chamber of Commerce is also an excellent way to learn the lay of the land. Most of them will provide information regarding shopping, entertainment, public transportation, and other amenities available to new residents.

Seek out the assistance of friends and family. When I represent my clients, I always try to market them first in those cities where they have friends and family. Look up people you knew in college, or network through your sorority or fraternity. Call your Aunt Helen and see if you can use her guest room for a month.

In my opinion, this is one of the best ways to go because it gives you a little more time and freedom in selecting an apartment that's right for you. In addition, you'll have a month to familiarize yourself with the city, and you'll have more time to accumulate enough money for your deposit and first month's rent. And perhaps most important, you'll be more comfortable because you are among friends and family.

Another option is to find a hotel or motel offering reasonable weekly rates. A lot of the expenses you incur in your job search and relocation are tax deductible. Don't forget to keep your receipts.

Getting moved is really not as bad as it may seem. Use your head. Use your available resources. And by all means, don't panic!

Your first few months on the job

Hurray for you! You got the job. Now you're the new kid on the block, so to speak, and you'll be going through a period of adjustment.

When my clients accept an offer, I spend some time preparing them for what they can expect once they go to work. For example, it'll be the first time most of you have been employed in a 9-to-5 position. That in itself can be a big adjustment. I'd like to offer a few suggestions that might help you adapt to your new environment and increase your chances for success.

1. **Be an observer.** Learn to listen to what's going on around you. When you start your career, there's a tremendous amount you can learn by simply keeping your ears open. You'll be taught the policies and procedures of the company during your orientation, but often you can learn equally as much simply by using your powers of observation and sharpening your listening skills.

2. **Don't become a clock watcher.** Your workday and hours will likely be structured during your initial training. As I mentioned earlier, it's probably your first 9-to-5 job. Don't get into the habit of walking in the door at 8:59 a.m., watching the clock for the noon hour, and then bolting out at 4:59 p.m. You don't want to be known as the employee who's last in and first out every day.

LOOKING AHEAD

Your performance and work habits will be scrutinized during your first few months on the job. Show up early, stay a little later, and don't live for the lunch hour. Your willingness to invest a little extra time in the job will ultimately pay off for you in earlier promotions and increased job responsibilities.

3. **Turn your back to office politics.** It'll take you a while to learn the pecking order of the management staff. Over time, you'll also discover which employees are favored and which ones aren't. And through observation, you'll eventually learn why one employee is favored over another.

   Promotions of middle and senior management people nearly always create some kind of a ripple effect. Things like who's going to be promoted to the newly created management opening, and why, are often discussed at the water cooler. Don't involve yourself in conversations like these. Keep your observations and opinions to yourself. You have nothing to gain and everything to lose by embroiling yourself in politically charged situations. You'll be a lot better off simply to observe and to learn from the mistakes of others.

4. **Don't gossip.** Just as I'm sure you don't want to be the topic of someone else's conversation when you're not around, you don't want to talk about others behind their backs. Things you say have a way of making it through the office grapevine. Establishing that type of a reputation could slow your chances for promotion or alienate you from other staff members.

5. **Identify with the winners.** It won't take you long to see who's doing the best job and experiencing the most success. Follow the examples they set, ask their advice when necessary, and model yourself after their performance.

   On the flip side, stay away from employees who have a negative attitude. You'll be able to spot those types rather quickly. It's very easy to get caught up in a gripe session over lunch. Even if you're not a negative type of individual, your association with that kind of employee could be damaging.

6. **Exercise patience.** Don't expect too much too soon. If you catch on quickly to the responsibilities of the job, that's great. But don't expect to get promoted when *you* think you're ready. The wheels that make corporations move, sometimes move more slowly than you'd like. Don't get frustrated or develop a bad attitude if you don't get what you want when you want it. Work hard and maintain a positive attitude and eventually you'll get what you deserve.

7. **Obey the rules.** Adhere to corporate policy, from the dress code on down the line to whether or not you're allowed to make personal phone calls during business hours. The company made the rule for a reason, so follow it.

8. **Don't date other employees.** Getting involved in a personal relationship with another employee, especially a manager, could prove to be your downfall. An office romance will stimulate gossip, create potential political problems, and might ultimately be a reason for terminating you.

9. **Get involved in extracurricular activities with the company.** A lot of corporations I work with encourage their employees to donate a few hours of their time each month to a charitable organization or a good cause, such as the Heart Association, local homeless shelters, the American Cancer Society, etc. If that's your company's policy, get active.

WAKE-UP CALL

Many companies have corporate-sponsored activities like softball teams, bowling leagues, picnics, and the like. Involving yourself in those types of activities opens the door for you to meet employees and managers of departments outside of your own. It's an excellent way of networking within the company and making your presence known.

10. **Ask for help if you're struggling with the training program or have a problem of any kind.** Don't be shy about going to your supervisor and saying you're having difficulties with the job. That's why they're there. It's not a good idea to keep your problem to yourself. You might fall behind in the training to the point where, out of exasperation, you throw in the towel.

    Managers are problem solvers. It's their primary function. Don't let a problem build into an unmanageable situation. As soon as you realize you're struggling, get the advice of someone who's walked that path and can help you work through the situation. Seeking out assistance is not a display of weakness, it's a display of strength.

11. **Treat your first year on the job like another year of college.**
When you're allowed to do so, take your training materials home and study them on your own time.

Supplement your corporate education by subscribing to and reading business periodicals related to the industry. By doing so, you'll increase the odds of completing your training ahead of schedule and securing that first promotion.

At this point, I'd like to say "Good Luck" to each and every one of you in your new career. But I won't. Luck won't have very much to do with your success. If you take everything you've learned and all the skills you've developed and then implement them, you will have a great deal of control over not only how far you go, but over how fast you get there. For those reasons, I instead offer my best wishes for your every earned success!

Index

About the Author

Linda Linn is a Certified Personnel Consultant and executive recruiter with Callos & Associates, a recruiting and placement firm. A highly regarded expert in the entry-level job marketplace, she has recruited for such companies as MCI, Campbell's, Roadway, Sherwin-Williams, and The Limited. She brings to this book a broad perspective that stems from her many years of experience both working with recruiters and hiring managers of Fortune 500 companies and interviewing, counseling, and placing entry-level job candidates. Linn is currently recruiting degreed professionals who are looking to make their first career move.